Blessed to be Skipped

Jocelyn Ali

Dedication

This book is dedicated to the man I call the "Hero of my life," my father. Thank you for being a great mentor, for showing me how to be a woman of character, for being an example for us, for teaching me to be a hardworking woman. Thank you for always being there for me, and the rest of all of us without any condition – your unconditional love towards us was unbelievable. I always recall one of your favorite phrases, "read books so your brain can open." I have never met a man like you in my life. I will be grateful all my life to God for you.

You were not only a great father but a great grandfather, brother, and son. You taught me not to give up and to always keep my head up, no matter the circumstance, to clean my tears and keep walking like nothing happened. I treasure when I am struggling, you encourage me to endeavor. No matter how old I got, you were always there for me anytime I needed you. The older we grew, the closer we became, take a moment back and look back at all the struggles we have come through from years back, but one thing you taught us was always to stay together close no matter the circumstance. Fathers like you are hard to find. My dancing partner, our Fridays were unbelievable, drinking and dancing was amazing, and your funny stories where all the kids used to laugh nonstop. Teaching the kids how to ride a bike and play basketball with them was something to be admired about you. You always worry about our wellbeing. Anytime I have something that bothers me, I call you right away, and you always give me the best advice. You always encourage me to learn and specially to read. Reading for you was number one. One thing about you is that you always walk around with a book on your pants back pocket.

Papi, you don't imagine how much "I LOVE YOU," no one can ever imagine. You are my first love. You dedicated your life to us, and I am grateful for that, and I will be my whole life and after. I will spend my whole life talking about what an amazing father I had. There are no words really to describe you. A father like you don't exist. Everyone has a "Hero" that they believe will save them. I have the best "Hero," and that is you because there will never be a "Hero" like you. "All I know is that you are the father anyone would wish to have."

Acknowledgment

First of all, I would like to say thank you, God, for giving me the strength to do this book. This is something that I always wanted to do since I was a child. I am very grateful to have the opportunity to accomplish something that I have dreamed of.

To the man who always supported me in all my crazy ideas, my husband. As much as I argue with you, you are always there for me, and I am very thankful and grateful for you to be part of my life, as, without your support, this would not be possible. My kids, who are the motor of my life, I can't be more than thankful and grateful to have both of you. One of the reasons I keep strong and never give up.

My firstborn, you taught me how to be a mother, and I give the best of me for you to be the man you are today, I am very thankful for all you accomplish throughout your journey of life.

My baby boy, I am so grateful to God for giving me the opportunity to be able to conceive once again another boy. You are a hand full, but every day I learn more and more that both of you are the best things that ever happened to me. There is nothing that I will change from either one of you because you guys are amazing just the way you are. I will always guide you both to the best of my knowledge and encourage you both to take the right path in this journey of life.

My sisters and brother, each of you have taught me so many things, one of them is the strength of a survivor, the other one is to be a fighter, and one more is to never give up. I admired you guys for that. My baby sister, thank you so much for being part of my life, you are such a brave person, and you teach me every day to be strong, and not to let anything defeat me. You are an inspiration of strength and courage.

To my niece and nephews who have shown me how fun it is to have all of them, thank you for being around my life. One of you taught me a big lesson that I will take with me all my life. My aunts and uncles who are always there for me, you guys have been a great mentor to me.

My cousins who are like sisters to me, to those who have been my shoulder and my advisor, thank you so much, I really appreciated everything from the bottom of my heart.

All the fun that we have together is priceless. To the ones that are no longer here, because God has called them, I miss you guys dearly.

To my childhood friend and my friends now thank you for that lasting friendship, we will be friends until life decides. I am thankful for you guys being part of my life. To those who come across my life unexpectedly, thank you, I have learned something from you. Last but not least, I would like to give special thanks to Paramount Ghostwriters for believing in my story and making my dream a reality. Thanks to the entire team who was always there any time I had a question or needed any additional help.

Furthermore, I can't be more than grateful towards Mrs. Davis Breshkai, who really makes me feel so comfortable in expressing myself and being who I really am. You are a really amazing human being and are always so kind. You always listen very carefully to every detail of my story. Thank you so much for that.

"Every day that we wake up is the beginning of a new day." I am very thankful to be able to wake up and continue my journey on this beautiful path called life. Don't take life for granted, appreciate every moment, whether it's good or bad. Each of them will teach us a lesson. Be thankful for everything, regardless of what it is. "This journey that's called life is full of surprises, take all of them as it's a SURPRISE."

About the Author

Jocelyn Ali was born in 1976. Her original name is Jocelyn Irene Vargas Rodriguez. She is a very passionate woman with big dreams. One thing she loves to do is take pictures. Jocelyn loves to create memories and she believes there is no better way. Her favorite animals are the horses because horses symbolize freedom and also represent power. Since she was a child, she used to say that one day, she will write her own story. Health is a major concern for her, and it's the number one thing that she is always concerned about, not only for herself but also for the people around her.

Jocelyn earned her Accounting degree and Business Administration in 1999. In 2003, she involved herself in Healthcare Management, and since then, she has been working to help communities in need of health care workers. In her free time, Jocelyn enjoys dancing, writing, and singing. Traveling is a must in her list, and she enjoys it gratefully with her family.

Six years ago, she created a page on Facebook on which she talks about rare diseases. Jocelyn has been educating families and kind of coaching them to clear their minds of misconceptions about how these diseases work in the human body. People from all over the world have approached her via message, and she is extremely satisfied with the outcome of the pages, despite the fact that it was a tremendous challenge for her to open such of page base. "Sometimes, the simplest things to one person could be the most difficult to others." In the future, Jocelyn would love to open a foundation to help others in need of guidance or assistance related to health.

Preface

This is a story about my life. A tale of how I had to watch my loved ones endure the sufferings that came with diseases. From first-hand experience, I can tell you that health is the most priceless element in your life. Nothing can give you your health back once you lose it. Only God can do that, so be grateful to God for all the times you have observed your health to be great.

My entire family struggled with a disease that caused cancers and tumors in their bodies. I lost most of my loved ones at the hands of it. However, something that I learned from all the losses that I suffered is that life goes on. You have to feel motivated and continue to live life helping others and yourself to maintain the optimum level of health. Never take your health for granted, and always be thankful for it by taking care of your body. Health is one of the greatest gifts given to us by God. So make sure to cherish it!

Contents

Page Left Blank Intentionally

Chapter 1
The Beginning

When walking through this journey called life, searching for its meaning and the point of being a part of this infinite universe, you encounter many ups and downs. I was always told that life is a rollercoaster back then. Frankly, I never thought about how it would be like to actually experience this ride, nor did I know that it would be one terrifying and devastating ride. I never knew that when this rollercoaster ride ends, your life ends too, until I lost my mother.

There are days in your life when you feel like you are in a garden where you have soft grass below your feet, beautiful flowers to pick from, and fresh air to breathe. You know, those days when you notice the bright, beautiful sky in the day and enjoy counting the stars when the sun goes down. However, there are days when you are afraid of the dark, you cannot wait for the night to go away, and the sun to finally rise. These are those days when you no longer enjoy counting the stars, you feel like the grass that felt smooth suddenly starts hurting your feet and you find it difficult to walk on it, you realize that the flowers that you picked have thorns and suddenly you find your fingers bleeding while the fresh air turns into a bad odor of fertilizers. While experiencing such days, I also learned that none of these days were permanent. There will be morning again, there will be happy days, and there will be sad days too but never a sad life.

During those days, when life is tough on you, that is when you learn your true strength and how much you can truly endure. No matter how hard it gets, do not lose hope in those days and keep believing that good days are on their way. You must always be grateful because you never know what life has in store for you.

Even though you experience things that challenge your faith and make you want to scream your lungs out, you can still be happy. Always remember that you are blessed to be alive, so no matter how difficult life gets, learn to appreciate little things. Gratitude can help you stay happy despite what you have been through, so always be grateful and learn to fall in love with life despite the hardships of life. There can be many things that could go wrong, but remember, you are blessed to be where you are.

Life is a blessing from God. If you have food to eat, a roof over your head, healthy parents, siblings you can share your entire day stories with, and people who care about you, you are blessed than millions and billions of people.

I am writing this book because I want people to realize how blessed they are to have the things that may be very tiny for them but could mean a world to someone else. Sometimes you may take certain things for granted, but what you don't realize is they could be a huge blessing for someone else. My goal in this book is to inspire others to trust their timing.

Some days we wake up and feel that life is perfect, and it couldn't be any better, but then all of a sudden, we get kicked out of that situation and start questioning why that happened. But believe me, when I say something even better is on its way, just do not lose hope.

In case you are wondering who I am, let me give a little background about myself. I live in the US, but I was born and raised in a different country. I was born in the Dominican Republic in the capital city of Santo Domingo. I grew up there until I was 15-years-old, and that's when we moved to the US. I grew up blessed with both my parents. I was their second child, and at that time, my father worked for a great company as a Mechanical Engineer. We are three sisters, including me, and a brother who is the youngest. I recall my father and my mother were very young back then. My mother was a housewife while my father was a mechanical engineer. He went to Europe to continue his studies and to be better in the field. His job was to supervise threading mechanical machines. Everything was going smoothly, and we were living a happy life.

I used to spend most of my time with my mother. I shared everything with her about my day, and she listened very patiently. I remember when I was a child, my mother told me that I was born with a bad heart condition. I couldn't breathe like a normal child, due to which I faced many problems.

Therefore, what she used to do was she would cover me in as little clothing as possible because she was scared that covering me in more clothes would suffocate me. She loved me a lot since I spent most of my time with her, and watching me having breathing issues was definitely something she would never take lightly. I had several checkups, and after running the tests, the doctors discovered that I had a hole in my heart. I was put on medications immediately when I was just a little child. The disease that I had is called heart murmur, and besides that, I had the main vein of my heart crossed; this condition is called transposition of valves. So, there had to be something done about it, and the doctors had to conduct surgery. My mother told me that when I was two-years-old, I became severely sick. My condition was so worse that I almost died. They had to rush me to the hospital immediately.

After the checkup, the doctors found out that the veins in my heart were jumbled, and they needed a transposition of my valves, which means they had to perform open-heart surgery on me. This wasn't something ordinary around the 70s, doctors rarely do an open-heart surgery as its risky, but they had to conduct mine so I could breathe properly and my blood could circulate to the other parts of the body.

Therefore, I was hospitalized in order to proceed with the surgery. My mother told me that when I came out of the hospital after the surgery and everything went well, she received a phone call from the doctors. They thanked us for hanging on so gratefully as well as they appreciated that I woke up, and everything was successful; however, I had to be on medication for the rest of my life. My uncle, at the time, was a medical student. He told his family that he was becoming a cardiac surgeon. He had a lot of connections, so he connected my mother and my father. He was a great part of the performance of my surgery and would explain to my parents how they were able to perform my surgery.

This happened back in 1978. During that time, not many people knew about this disease. Back in the Dominican Republic, which is a third world country, I was the first child to have open heart surgery in my family, and this was a huge piece of news for everyone, and they were all going crazy. As a result, oftentimes, my room would be full of people coming to see me.

At the end of the day, everything went well, and I was saved from death, but it left a huge scar on my back. The scar that I still carry with myself today, beginning from the middle of my back, it runs all the way up and connects with my left breast.

I still recall my mom telling me that she used to leave the back of my clothes open because she didn't want me to feel that it is something that should be hidden and be embarrassed about. She wanted me to embrace it so nobody would have the guts to say anything about it. However, most importantly, she did it mainly because she did not want me to feel uncomfortable or ashamed. She wanted me to feel confident regardless of the scar.

That is something I appreciate about my mother the most that she created so much comfort for me that I was able to show my back freely despite the scar.

She always made me feel that I was blessed to be able to survive. Though there were times I used to feel embarrassed about the scar when people used to ask me about it. I would always remain blank and quiet because I would never know how to answer that question.

I remember one day I was so done that I ran to my mom, put my arms around her, and cried a river. She asked me what was wrong, and I told her how people always made fun of me. They asked me what is it that I have on my back and what happened to me, and I would always remain silent. My mother's older sister was also there, witnessing all this, she said to me that *tell them you are blessed, tell them the mark that you have on your back is a blessing from God.*

Her words somehow encouraged me, and I started feeling confident about it. So, whenever anyone asked me about it, that's what I used to tell them. I would proudly tell people that it is a blessing from God. The reason behind them not telling me what it was, was because my mother never wanted to go in details of what really happened. Therefore, I did not know much about what had happened to me at the time.

My mother always treated me like I was some sort of fragile princess. I could never imagine my life without her, but life had a lesson to teach me. When I was just five-years-old, my mother became very sick. Being a child who was very close to her mother, this was no less than a nightmare. I became numb, and the fear of losing my mother took birth inside me.

I had no one to share how I felt about my mother's sickness, so I used to write them down in a diary. This was the only way I was able to cope with myself, I had to vent my feelings out in order to feel lighter, so I used to write them down. As a result, I continued doing that as I grew up; whatever happened in my life, I used to write it down on a piece of paper.

Hence, this book is something I always wanted to write since I was a child.

When you are little, I don't know if it's the culture of the country you are living in or some other reason, sometimes you cannot go and talk to an adult. At least for me, that's how it was. I couldn't express my anxiety, my anger, and my sadness of seeing my mother sick to anyone in my family. I was very little for all that I was experiencing, so I used to write in order to refrain from all those feelings.

My mother was going through pregnancy and knew nothing about the disease that had taken birth inside her. The time had come, and they rushed my mother to the hospital. No one knew about my mother's sickness until she gave birth to my little brother. That's when she had surgery, and that's when doctors discovered my mother was very sick.

My mother faced lots of difficulties while giving birth to my little brother. The doctors had to undertake an emergency C-section in order to save both the lives. When they opened my mother's womb, they noticed that her womb was full of tumors, but they did not know what to exactly do at the moment, so they took the baby out and closed the womb again. My mother did not know what was going on. The doctors had only informed my father about it, and my father informed my mother's sister and his brother, who was a doctor, that my mother was sick and there was nothing at the moment they could do for her. We were only three sisters, and our little brother was just born. I remember at that time we used to live in a really nice neighborhood and a very beautiful home. I recall that day, and I remember how excited my father was that my mother was going to give birth to another baby. Everybody was happy and excited about the newborn baby.

My brother was the first male child in the family, so everyone was excited. My father threw a huge party to welcome my brother into the house. He did not say anything to my mother because we all were so happy to have a little addition to our family. He didn't want to ruin things for my mother. At that time, I was only five-years-old, so I did not really know what was going on, but I knew there was something that my family was keeping from me.

If I talk about myself, I am naturally very curious, and I pay a lot of attention to my surroundings. So, I always tried to listen to what was going on around the house. As I said earlier, I was attached to my mother, so I had this feeling that there was something wrong with her. This was driving me crazy, but I was so young that I could not help her. I felt helpless. A few days later, my mother was rushed to the hospital again because she was not feeling well. The doctors immediately took her in the operation theatre and again opened her womb to see whether they could do something about it. I remember my father and my aunt talking that there was nothing they could do to save my mother from the disease. My mother was very sick. She had cancer. So, they opened my mom's womb only to close it back in dismay.

My mother still did not know what was going on. Back in the 1980s, the doctors used to hide from the patients what their condition was. They always used to tell their family, so only my father knew what was exactly going on with my mom. My mother only knew that she was sick; she had no clue how severe her sickness was. My father loved my mother a lot. He always used to tell her not to worry and that they will do everything possible to help her.

All of this reminded me of how my mother never told me what had happened to me when I was just a little child and how she always encouraged me. A year later, when I was six-years-old, I witnessed my mom becoming very different than how she was just a year before she got sick. She was even sicker now and continuously running to hospitals. She would make it to the hospital, but again, they would send her back home without being able to do anything. I started noticing that there was something really wrong with her. Besides everything, my mother was a very strong woman. I never saw her crying or complaining. She was surviving through a deadly disease; still, she never made any of us feel that she was weak. She didn't want us to feel pity for her.

My father was flowing all his savings like water while paying for household expenses back in the Dominican Republic. Paying for the expenses of such a severe disease was like a luxury back in the '80s, it was not everyone's cup of tea. We were not a very rich family to be able to provide for so many expenses, but my father always managed everything without saying a word.

She was so sick that going through the radiations and all the chemotherapies they performed barely had any positive impact on her health, and it perforated her colon. Due to the severe condition, they had to remove a part of her colon, and she had a colostomy bag.

So, imagine you are as young as six-years-old, and you are supposed to have a normal body, and you see that your mother has to put on a bag on her stomach. That left a huge impact on me. When you witness somebody close to you getting a transformation like that, it leaves you stunned and confused. I didn't understand what was going on, but I knew for sure that my mother was very sick.

It made me feel so bad that I never wanted to leave her alone in the hospital. Every time she was admitted, I would go to her room and hide myself somewhere so my father couldn't see me and take me back home. I did this just so that I could stay with my mom a little more.

My mom used to tell my father and my youngest aunt not to worry. But I was not going anywhere. I wanted to stay with my mom because I did not know for how long she was going to stay there, and I did not know for how long I would be able to see her breathing. Thinking she was not going to be there anymore scared me to death, therefore I wanted to give her all the time that I had.

One of the doctors would always tell me that it was not safe for me to stay there, and I should go home, but I was persistent. I used to even skip school so that I could stay with my mom at the hospital. I loved learning new things, and I believe I was gifted this by my mother. She loved learning new things and was always involved in learning art and crafts. She used to sew clothes herself, and because of that, she made our clothes herself along with curtains, blankets, and other things. As a matter of fact, she even used to decorate our house, all thanks to her creativity.

Other than that, she was a great dancer. She loved dancing, and salsa was her favorite dance form. She looked beautiful and elegant whenever she danced with my father. I used to love watching them dance. I always describe her as an amazing person and the most talented mother. My younger years with her were the best years of my life, even though she was sick at that time.

My mother was very much attached to her family, so she used to visit her siblings regularly. She had four siblings, three sisters, and one brother. Her parents died during mid-ages when they were young in their '60s or '70s. From her father's side, she had more brothers and sisters; therefore, she loved to go and pay them a visit.

I remember when I was a child, we used to get dressed and meet her side of the family. She loved it whenever she saw her complete family together. The neighborhood we lived in was quite far from where our family members lived, and so we always used to be accompanied by my aunt because the school that my sisters and I went to was close to my aunt's house. Thus, every day after school, we would go to our aunt's house, and my mother used to pick us up. As soon as my brother was born, we moved to another neighborhood for some reason. I still don't know what reason, but this new place proved to be even worse for us.

Few years after moving to this new neighborhood, my older sister was kidnapped when she was only 14-years-old by a guy who was in his 20s. It was another night of tragedy for the family. I recall that night was horrible for all of us. My mother didn't know how to tell my father about it. I was eight years old at the time. I recall my mother asked my youngest sister and me to look for her everywhere, but we were not able to find her.

My mother started panicking, and she didn't know what to do. She asked me to go and look for my sister. At this point, my mother's body was weak because of so many tumors in her body, and now, due to the perforation of her colon, her body was a little bent. She was unable to walk straight, and she was in a lot of pain. That is why I remember my mother asking me to go look for my sister at the store. I was young back then, and this new neighborhood was not safe at all. I felt so bad at times for my mother's helplessness, and the worst part of it was watching her look older than she actually was. My mother lost her consciousness. Suddenly, my heart skipped a beat. It was as if the world had stopped. Watching her lying on the floor like that, I thought this was it, the moment I was afraid of the most. I went hysterical, and I couldn't speak. I thought my mother died, and I was going crazy. Thanks to the neighbors who helped my mother regain her consciousness. The great thing was that my sister was found safe the next day.

The reason why I brought this up is that this happened when my mother was really sick. To me, it was terrifying, and I recall saying, *"My mother does not need more stress, she is so sick already."* Since the doctors were unable to remove any tumors from her body, therefore her body started to deteriorate. The doctors were trying hard, doing everything that was possible for my mother to survive.

At this point, she was getting continuous radiations and chemotherapies. The doctors did everything possible so that my mother could live. The incident of my sister getting kidnapped left a huge impact on my life. I never imagined what it would be like if any of my siblings were not there anymore. I was too juvenile for it, but I really felt the pain of knowing that your sister is alive, but you cannot be with her or see her because someone took her away from you. So, what exactly happened was my mother sent my sister to a nearby store. Since my mother was sick and she had trouble walking, my sister had to go alone to buy accessories related to her school project that she had to bring to school the next day. We went to a Catholic school, and when you go to a Catholic school, you have to do a lot of things; they help you become creative.

I remember that day like it happened just yesterday. My sister went to the shop alone, and the rest of my siblings and I were busy doing the random stuff. Suddenly my mother looked at the clock and realized that it had been two hours since my sister went to the shop and hadn't returned yet. She was supposed to be back in less than half an hour.

After this, everyone in my family bonded together to look for clues and find out where my sister could be. We called the police, and they started investigating immediately. The entire night was spent with us panicking, and finally, with the help of the police, my sister was found the next day. The guy who kidnapped her was then arrested. Later, we got to know that he was actually my sister's boyfriend. That's something that I still remember today, and that taught me that when you love somebody, you may feel free and safe with that person. They both were so young, and my sister was only 14-years-old. They were too young for all this; she did not realize what she was getting herself into. Since I was very observant, all these things stayed in my head, and I used to tell myself, *I will never allow anything like that to happen to me.*

Whatever that had happened left an impact on our lives, and we decided to move from this new neighborhood too. My father moved us to a new house, and it was so beautiful. We were the first family who moved in there.

We all were so happy that we left that depressing neighborhood with all the bad memories, and were very much excited about the new and beautiful house that we got to live in. It was like a fresh start for all of us. However, my mother was still sick, and the new neighborhood was not convenient for my mother's sickness because transport was not accessible in that area, and we had no means of traveling available nearby. Let's say if my mother got sick in the middle of the night, there was no ambulance nearby to call.

There was no such emergency number that could come to the house immediately and transport the patient to the hospital. Since we were too young and my father was mostly away due to work, they decided to take my mother to her sister's home, where there was transportation available so if anything was to happen to my mother, they had access to a car as well as the hospital since it was nearby.

That was another heartbreak for me and something that I had to adjust with. However, before they took my mother away to her sister's, I spent a beautiful time with my mother. I would try my best to only stick to my mom when home. My older sister used to go to school in the morning, and my younger sister and I used to go to school in the afternoon, so I was always home in the morning. My mother couldn't cook because she was getting chemotherapies, so she used to teach me how to cook.

I was around eight-years-old, and I was learning to cook at that age. My mother used to sit on a chair because of the radiation and all the therapies that she was going through; therefore, she was not allowed to go near heat as that could make her sicker. So, my mom used to teach me the basics of cooking, as well as she used to tell me how much water I should pour in the pan and all the ingredients that I had to put in. Whatever I made; she would patiently tell me how to make it. I am so grateful that I got to live those days with my mom when for a little while, she forgot about her disease and taught me how to cook. I remember that she was always observing me and telling me how much I have to put down so that I do not get burned. She would continuously tell me to be careful and take care of the little things.

I always wanted to be close to her and learn things from her as much as I could. I was the child who never said no to my mom. I didn't care about the outside world; I was happy in my own little world where there was me and my mom. I did not care about going outside to play like all the other kids. I just wanted to stay at home with her.

My childhood was very different, as compared to most kids. It wasn't the kind of childhood where I got into fights with my friends or random kids, and I never went on cycling outside when all the elders had their evening tea. The reason was that I was always with my mom. I used to say to her, *"Oh my God! Look at my friends playing, but I don't care because I want to be with you."* She used to tell me to go out and play, and I used to say, *"No, I want to stay with you,"* so this way, I was always with her. I used to go with her everywhere she went, and since my younger brother was very little, she used to carry him with herself as well. I used to get jealous of my little brother because he was the only boy my mother had, so she adored him a lot. I didn't want to share her with anyone, not even my own little brother.

I always tried my best to help my mother in every way possible. I helped her with everything she needed. I remember I hated going to school because I saw it as a separation from my mother, and the thought of not being with her made me sad. I was not doing really well in school because I was always thinking about my mother's sickness. At times I would find myself unable to concentrate on anything for a long time.

Everything has an ending, and this beautiful time had to come to an end. The time was here, and they took my mom to her sister's house, leaving all of us behind. After this, things became worst. I remember my younger sister used to go to school in the morning, and the rest of us used to stay back with my father and leave when my father left. It was a very difficult time for all of us, and we did not know if things could get any worse.

My father was the only one earning, and even though our other relatives were always ready to help, my father was very responsible and always said that my mother was his responsibility, not anyone else's.

They were a very young couple dealing with such a problem. When my mother was sick, she was only 29-years-old while my father was just 30-years-old. My father was very handsome. He had a muscular body, and although he was not very tall, he was really attractive. It would not be wrong if I say he was very sexy and full of life. I remember he used to flirt with a lot of girls when I was younger.

There was a woman who was always after him since my father was a great dancer and had an elegant personality. He used to dance like a professional. I remember my mother telling my father that she really wanted him to leave her because she was so sick and she hated it. Since my father was such a nice-looking man, she wanted my father to be free and have another wife. However, my father clearly refused and said, *"No, I am going to stay here with you until the end, and I am not going to leave."*

These are the things I used to hear because of the curious soul that I have. I listened to everything very carefully while my other sisters minded their own business, playing and doing the routine activities. I paid great attention to everything that happened around the house and especially around my mother.

I was always home, even though my mother was not there, and my sister was always outside playing. The main thing that I recall about my neighborhood is that most of the houses were not gated. Our house couldn't be gated because my father didn't have enough money to install a gate and had other expenses to take care of. Since they couldn't afford even the windows, they hired a guard. He was always around the house so nobody could enter.

One evening I was home alone. I remember it was a very nice house with three bedrooms and one bathroom. There was an area outside where you could do your laundry or whatever you wanted to do; however, the area was not covered. I don't remember exactly what I was doing in that area when I heard some footsteps. I thought it was my sister so I turned around to see and I saw a boy standing there. I was only around 8-years-old, and that boy must be around 15 or 16 years old.

If I describe myself, I have very fair skin, and I always had long dark black hair. My mother always told me that I was the most beautiful girl in the world. So, this boy just entered the house out of nowhere, and before I could do anything or call the guard, he pushed me to the wall, put his hand tightly around my mouth so that I don't shout, and almost tried to rape me. I was fighting hard, I protested, but nobody was there to rescue me from this teenage beast, and I was the only one who could save myself.

But even after all this, I was so strong because of my mother. When my mother was sick, she used to talk to me a lot, while giving me pieces of advice. I always used to ask her why she would tell me such things, and she would cover it up by saying because you had surgery at a very early age.

One thing I remember is that she always used to tell me that, *always be strong and never give in to your situation*. I used to take a lot of pills every month along with monthly injections to prevent any infections in the body because if I get an infection in my body and it goes to my heart, I die.

So, she was always bringing a lot of attention to it, making sure I was getting my medications on time. Every month they used to put a pill under my tongue so she would always say things like, *make sure you get your pills every morning, take care of yourself, stay safe, despite the heart condition that you have, never lose hope, and be so strong that nobody can walk on you. You always have to be strong. The things that happened to your sister should not happen to any of you.*

She used to teach me so many things and advised me so many things that I was so sure that I was not going to let anything happen to me because I wanted my mother to be proud of me. I constantly thought about everything she told me. Those words of hers were engraved in my head, and I always had this thing in my mind that I couldn't let anything happen to myself.

Getting back to the horrible incident, I was all alone in the house, and I fought with this guy so much until I escaped from him. I ran into the house, and he ran after me. He tried to catch me and ripped my clothes. I ran into the house and closed the door.

I was able to get him out of the house, and I don't know from where the strength came in me, but I fought him bravely and threw him out of the house. I took anything that I could get my hands on and threw it on him. I beat him up and threw a knife at him. Everything that I found, I took it and threw it at him. I think I had the strength to fight him because I hold on to the words my mother used to say; *Don't let anybody ever use you. Don't let anybody hurt you. Fight until you can*, and that's exactly what I did. That's all I have in my head. If you have to throw anything on anybody in order to save yourself, do it!

My father used to say the same things to us because we were three girls and one little boy. He used to say, *don't let anybody do anything to you and fight until you can. Even if you couldn't fight, at least you did everything that you could.*

Therefore, I fought him until I was able to get him out of the house. I don't recall how I did that; I just have the image of this guy in my head and how I fought him. He was very slim and very skinny. He was not tall, and I had so much strength that I threw a chair, a knife, and everything that I found.

I started screaming and yelling my lungs out, and to my misfortune, nobody heard me. I got him out of the house, keeping in mind that my windows had no gate and no bars, nothing. So, he kept entering the house, once through the front and once through the side. Like if I threw him out of the front door, I forgot the side door, and he came through it, and I was fighting again. He put me on the floor, continued ripping my clothes, but I don't know how but I was able to get him off again, and I was able to close the door and lock it. It was something very weird that I was yelling, and nobody was listening to me; not a single soul heard me.

Every room that I entered, he was by the window yelling ugly words at me like, *you are not going to be safe. Don't worry. I'm going to get you. I'm going to rape you. You're going to be mine. I love your body; you look so good. I am going to eat you* and so many ugly vulgar things. He was seventeen, and I was only eight. All that I had in my mind was, *I don't know anything about what's going on, and I am only worried about my mother, who is sick and dying.*

Thankfully, he did not rape me. We fought for hours, but he did not touch my body and did not do anything bad to me. Although he threatened me, thank God he failed at it. The saddest part of it all is that I never told my father about it. I never told anyone until I was older. I did not tell my father because he was so protective of us that if I told him, he would have killed that boy and would have ended up in jail.

I was only eight-years-old, and all I was thinking was what would happen if I tell my father, if he killed that guy and ended up in jail, then what would happen to my mom? Who will help her? Who will take care of her? Who will be her support? We are too juvenile to work, so who is going to earn? Where will the money come from to help treat my mother's sickness? That way, my mother is not going to survive because we need money to help her. These were the things that were running through my head and became a seal outside my mouth.

When my sister came back home that day after playing and saw me panicking, I just covered it up, saying I was feeling sick due to my heart condition. She believed me, and after that, I did not bother telling anyone. I stayed quiet.

The guy who tried to rape me used to live in my neighborhood. He was wealthy and belonged to a very rich family. Every time he used to see me, he would give me signs that he was going to rape me. He would make weird sexual gestures, but I had to ignore him. As a result, this made me never want to go outside. I was always careful and always inside my house. I did not want to give him another chance. I was so afraid that something was going to happen to me that I decided to only go out when I would be accompanied by my sister or father. What we used to do is we would leave the house early in the morning, my sister used to go to school, and I used to stay at my aunt's where my mother was until midnight. We used to come back home when my father returned in the night around 12'o clock. We would move back and forth, and that's how life was rolling us. The struggle that we went through due to my mother's sickness cannot be imagined.

Despite everything, I believed in good days and that things would get better, that my mother would get better and everything would be alright soon. I will be able to play outside like normal kids and make new friends. However, since I was always with my mom, I started going to church. The neighbors that we had next door had a church inside their home.

I used to say to my mom to let me take the kids to the church, and she would agree, so that's how we used to go the church where I used to cry and pray to God to help my mom because I always heard everyone saying that God would help and He would make things right, so I was only trying to seek His help. I started going to church regularly and kept praying, but with each passing day, she got sicker. I used to say to God why He was not listening to me. There came a point in life when I stopped believing in God. I stopped praying.

I used to stay at my aunt's house the entire day. My mother used to have her own bedroom, and she used to have a hospital bed. When you have cancer, and it gets severe while spreading all over your body, your body starts to smell really bad. My mother's odor of sickness was there, but I did not care about it at all, and I wanted to stay with her. I remember when she was really sick and almost dying, she said to me:

"When I die, I want you to continue taking the pills for your heart. Remember you have a brother and sisters and they need you. I want you to guide them the right way. I want you to support them and always be there for them. You're going to be a special great mother. You are going to be a great mother because look how much you are attached to me; you are not even going outside to play."

And I used to say, *"No, mom, don't worry, you are going to be fine."* My mother used to have a Bible next to her, and even though I was upset with God, I used to help her pray, thinking He would listen to her and accept her prayers. They say God always responds to our prayers. I thought God was not listening to me because I was so young back then and that He would listen to my mother because she's older. I was under the impression that when you are young, nobody listens to you.

That is why I started writing because I believed that you are the only one who will listen to yourself. I started writing because that is the only way I had to express myself. I was writing every day when my mother was sick about everything that she was going through. I recall the day when my mother died. I remember it was Saturday, but the night before that day, my mother did not look good. At this point, she was drained and had become very skinny.

Apart from that, I learned from my mom what strength is. She was so strong, and even though she was so sick, she always wanted to look beautiful. She used to tell my aunt to comb her hair. She asked her hair to be cut very short so that they would be easier to manage. She had trouble moving, nor could she walk anymore. She couldn't get off from the bed because the tumor had ripped her skin and came out of her belly. The segment where my mom had the colostomy bag,

I could see the tumor on her stomach, and I used to think about how that could happen to a human being. How can anyone be deteriorated like this? I did not care, regardless of what her body looked like. I still loved her. The day before she died was Friday. My aunt and my father were together in the house, praying. My father was so loving to my mother. He was an amazing husband. I used to say that when I would get married, I would make sure that I would marry a guy exactly like my father.

He used to go to her in the morning before he would drop us to school, to give my mother a bath, make sure she was clean and smelled good despite the disease, and make sure that she had everything she wanted. If he did not have the money for that, he used to look for the money to make sure that my mother had everything that she needed. I wanted someone to love me like that when I got older, someone who would protect me the way my father protected my mother and all of us.

On that Friday night, we were all there, but my mother was not talking anymore. She was agonizing. She asked me to come close to her, and she whispered in my ear, *"You are going to be such a great mother."* Before we went home, she told my older sister to take care of her siblings, although she had said the same things to me, she told my older sister as well because she was the oldest.

I remember she was telling her that *"you are going to be in charge, so you have to protect them. Make sure your sister is okay, don't give her any stress because you know if she gets stressed, she will pass out and end up in a hospital."* That was the last thing she told my older sister. I don't remember her saying anything to my younger sister and my brother at the time.

I was always focused on my little brother. With time, I got very attached to him. Earlier, I used to get jealous of him because he was the only son my mother had since she wanted a son so badly. Unfortunately, she did not get to live with him, she did not get to raise him, and she did not get to play with him because of her condition. When my brother was little, he wanted to be outside playing – he did not get to be with my mother either and did not really know her. I always feel blessed that I at least got to live and know this beautiful and amazing human I call 'mom.'

Chapter 2
Childhood Years

The day of good-bye had finally come, the day that was definitely not awaited, the day I dreaded the most, the day I lost my mother, forever.

It was five o'clock in the morning when I felt some uneasiness in the house. I could hear the distinct chattering because I was not in a very deep sleep. It was so white outside that one could not see anything. My aunt had come to get my father in an emergency. I remember when my father left, for some reason, I woke up. As soon as I woke up, I came outside the room, and my older sister was standing there.

She seemed tense, but the first thing she said to me was, *"take your pill,"* to which I replied, *"Why do I have to take the pill? I don't take it so early."* And she said, *"Take your pill. I want you to take your pill because mommy told me to give it to you early today"* Saying that she put the pill under my tongue, but I was very alert. I could sense there was something very wrong. I told her, *"Don't lie to me. Tell me the truth. Did mommy die?"* She immediately replied, as if trying to cover the truth, *"No, no. Just get dressed, and we are going to see mommy."* She assured me that nothing had happened. I was still not at peace, I insisted her to tell me the truth, and she denied again saying that mom is okay.

So, we all got dressed, I had put on a pink dress, and when I came out, my sister said, *"No, don't wear that dress, it is a very bright color."* I replied, *"So what? I can wear anything that I want."* She replied strictly, *"No, I want you to wear something calmer and not so bright."* I could not understand why was she saying such things when mommy was okay, so I cried out, *"Why? Tell me, is she dying?"* and she again covered it up, saying everything was fine, but I was so sure that it was not.

So, we were all dressed, sitting on the porch, in the front of the house, waiting for our aunt to come and pick us up. My sister said to me, *"Don't worry! I am always going to be here for you. Everything is going to be fine. I am going to become a woman in the house. I know that you know how to cook because your food is so good and I love it, mommy said the food you make is very delicious, and she taught you how to cook."* My older sister did not know how to cook because she was at school in the morning till two o'clock; therefore, I was at home with my mom, and I was the second oldest. She said, *"You are going to be cooking by yourself now, and we all will eat the food that you make."* And I was like, *"Why are you saying that?"* and she still did not tell me what was exactly going on. My sister was only 14-years-old, so she really did not know how to hide it.

After a while, my aunt came to pick us up and took us to her place, where mommy was staying. I can never forget that day from the moment we were taken to the funeral to the moment we came back. When we reached, I saw a lot of people gathered at my aunt's house. My youngest aunt was there too, who was very much attached to my mother because she was such a lovely lady.

Anyone who met my mother, they could not help but love her. Anybody I talked to about my mother, they used to say great things about her. I am not saying all this because my mother is dead. I am saying this because I learned this from her. I have witnessed on my own that how great of a human she was. How she took care of all of us and how she stayed strong despite such a tragic disease.

I can never forget the morning and the exact time my mother died. It was Saturday, January 23rd, 1987, exactly at eleven thirty-three in the morning when my uncle pronounced my mother's death to everyone present. His words were like a huge mountain that had just broken down on me. I felt like my life was over. My body started to shiver, and I felt as if the whole world has run out of light. All of a sudden, it was all dark, and my mind was blank.

I froze for a few moments. The only thing that I managed to do was that I grabbed my brother, who was only four-years-old at the time, and quickly went outside. Without a thought, I started running on the streets while tightly holding my brother. I did not know what I was doing and why I was doing so. I had no control over my actions. My mind was unable to think. I was just running blindly with tears flooding through my eyes.

A lady from the neighborhood saw us and immediately called out my name – she shouted and somehow managed to stop me from running. She politely asked me, *"Jocelyn, what's going on? Why are you running?"* I was crying so bad by then that the only thing I managed to say was *"My mother just died."*

Of course, everyone knew my mother. She knew my mother was sick but barely knew what my mother was going through. Even though I was too young, I assumed I knew exactly what my mother had and what she died of. The lady took us back home. When you're young, and somebody dies, nobody cares about you. Nobody gives a shit about how you feel. Nobody would come to you and say I am so sorry this happened to you. None of the condolences are for you. They are only for adults. People do feel sorry for you and look at you with sympathy like now you don't have a mother.

All they cared about was what was going to happen to us because, at this point, when my mother died, my father was young for his age. My mother was 34-years-old, and my father was 35. Without thinking, everyone was just talking about what is going to happen and that he is probably going to find another woman. My mother had just died, and people had the audacity to talk about such things.

My entire family was devastated, and I could not believe that people could be this cruel. My younger sister was so nervous about my mother's demise that she was continuously laughing, nonstop, as if trying to heal herself through the laughter, as if trying to avoid everything and believe that things were good. I was so angry because I didn't understand back then what was wrong with her. Our mother left this world, and she was laughing like she had lost her senses. I remember there was somebody holding her because she couldn't stop laughing. That was her reaction to what had happened. I looked for my older sister, and I found her banging her head against the wall.

It was all so painful to picture that I wished that it had never happened. I wished things could go back to how they were before. I wished my mother was breathing again, no matter if she was sick, at least she was there for us, making us a complete family, guiding us through things we knew nothing about. Everything seemed so different now, and I felt that we are never going to be happy again. I could not help but think about what was going to happen next.

The whole family started preparing for the funeral. When we have funerals in our country or most of the countries, we don't wait for anything and immediately start the preparations. We wear black or white. It's nothing more than that. I remember that Saturday when my mother passed away. Each moment is still fresh in my memory like it just happened yesterday. They got all the arrangements right away and took my mother to the funeral home and got the things prepared. Since my little brother was too young, they did not allow him to enter. Letting him have that memory of my mother being in a casket could have had a very negative impact on his entire life. Therefore, my little brother and my cousin were left outside with my grandfather.

I had never left my mother's side ever since I was a little child. I was so attached to her, and it was so hard for me to believe she was no more, and I had to let her go. I wanted to stick to her for one last time. While everybody was busy in the funeral rituals, I took a chair inside the funeral home and sat next to the casket. I sat there for hours and never moved from there the entire time.

I remember that dreadful evening moment by moment. Everyone was crying. It was a huge shock for all of us. I felt so sorry for my father. He had nobody to express exactly how he felt. My older sister was continuously trying to open the casket, and she was shaking. She kind of fell on my mother, and the next moment I remember is that I was screaming because I thought my mother was getting hurt. It was like a never-ending nightmare for me, and things were only getting worse.

I was just sitting there, staring at my mom without blinking. I can never forget her expressions when she passed away. I will always have that face in my memory. She looked sick yet calm as if finally, relieved from all the pain she had borne for years. The next thing I will always remember is the way people looked at my siblings and me with so much sadness as if our entire lives were over, and that was somewhat true.

Who was I going to look up to? How would my life go on without her? What was going to happen to me? What would happen to my siblings? There were many questions popping up in my head with no possible answer, while I was sitting next to the casket, which contained her dead body.

While we were there, an aunt from my mother's side that I never met in my life showed up out of nowhere. She started saying things like she was going to take one of us with herself. Either my younger sister, or myself, or maybe both of us. She owned a "save the children" organization, so she thought we were going to be better living with her. Since my father was young, she thought he was going to give his children away. Little did she know how much my father loved my mother and how obsessive he was regarding all of us. However, her words had the ability to scare me. She added to the pain I was already enduring. My mind was losing its balance, thinking that I lost my mother, and now I would have to live without my father. My mind was racing simultaneously with my heart, *we are going to get separated, and I am never going to see him again. I am not going to see my little brother and my older sister anymore.* All of these things were going through my mind, and I felt like I was going to go crazy.

The funeral was finally over. They usually last the entire day from the morning until the night. So, at night, we went back to our aunt's house where my mother was staying. I went straight to the room where she passed, and I just sat there next to her bed, trying to feel her presence. But I couldn't cry. I couldn't express myself. While there was a storm of words and tears inside, I was calm on the outside. Everything was just inside, so I found it best to pour it all out on a paper.

One of my aunts found me sitting there in her room and told me to come to them. In my head, I was like, why do I have to leave this room? This is the only thing I am left with. This is the place where my mother used to be all the time, the place where I came to meet her every day. In my mind, her spirit was there. I felt like she was probably around, and she was going to listen to me. But I had to come out of that room. The next morning again, it was Sunday, January 25th, 1987. We went back to the funeral home, and everyone was there. The whole family was again giving all the condolences to the adults and nothing to the children.

That's one thing I want to highlight and say to the adults that children do have feelings too, and they need attention at such moments. Just give them a hug; they need it more than anything. Show them you care and tell them that everything is going to fine. Don't act like they are not going to be affected just because they are children.

When we are young, we have feelings, we are fragile, and we need love and affection more than adults do. Children who have lost someone at such a young age want to feel secure because they have lost someone that was so important to them. Even though I knew everything was going to be fine, however, at the moment, I felt that as if someone had crushed my whole world beneath their foot. I needed someone to wrap me in their arms and comfort me with words.

The funeral came to an end. The other family members were leaving, and again I went back to the house, straight to the room I was pulled out from because they thought I shouldn't be there.

The next day which was January 26th, 1987, early in the morning, it was the time my mom was going to be buried. Everyone was there. The morning felt like a dark night in disguise. When they took my mother down into the grave, it was like a nightmare. I could not believe that I would never see her again. That was it, I will never be able to feel her presence, and I will never be able to hold her again. That was the last time I was seeing her, and I could not even see her because they covered the casket, they put her six feet down and started covering her with dirt.

It was so hard because I could not tell anyone how I felt exactly. I could not express myself; I couldn't cry. My tears were dropping from my eyes, but I couldn't scream like I wanted to. I wanted to scream at God and ask Him why He took her away so soon. It was the worst thing in my life, seeing that my mother would not be there with me anymore. Everything was over. We went back to the house. In my culture, where I come from, which is the Spanish culture, when someone passes away, we start counting nine days from the day the person was buried. During those nine days, we pray a lot for the departed soul every day before we go to the church. In my mother's case, we grew up Catholic, so we were regularly going to the church. Therefore, every day for nine days, our house was full of people.

I felt like the sky had fallen on me. Everything seemed to have stopped. My life felt empty, and with each passing day, I missed my mother even more. Every day in those nine days, I would sit quietly in the corner and not talk to anyone. Every morning my sister used to come with a pill and keep it under my tongue. The medication I was taking due to the condition of my heart used to help keep me calm as well.

I used to think that's how my mother wanted me to be, and my sister was taking well care of that. She was making sure I was taking my medication on time.

On the last day of the prayer, which was the ninth day, my mother's sister, our aunt, said something to us that I will never forget to this date. The ninth is a big day; a lot of people come to say the last good-bye to the spirit. All my siblings and I were wearing white dresses with black ribbons. Our aunt came to the three of us sisters and said, *"I don't want you guys to cry. I don't want you guys to act abnormally because the house will be full of people. If you want to cry, you have to go in the room, cover your mouth with a pillow, and cry as much as you want."*

Her words were like thorns. They have stuck to my heart, and I will always feel the pain I felt at that very moment. I mean, I could not believe how insensitive one could be. To me, it was horrible.

How can you tell me not to cry for my mother, who died a few days ago? You are telling me to hold my feelings just because you don't want people to see me cry. How brave of you to say that to my sisters and me.

As the years went by, I forgave her because I probably understood it was possible. She did not want anyone to say anything, but still, it was cruel of her to say that to a child.

Through this book, I want to say, on behalf of every child that has to go through such a painful tragedy, losing a parent is not something everyone can endure. It is the most challenging phase, especially for a child, so please be kind to them. Show them that you love them and that you care about them. If only one person cares enough to ask them if they are okay, I believe that would be enough for them because, in our case, we had no one. Don't tell the child to hold their feelings, let the child cry, and if they want to scream, let them scream. That is how he is going to take that out. Let them grieve and bring that pain out of themselves. Don't let them bottle up their emotions because it can leave a negative impact on their entire life. They won't be able to speak their feelings for the rest of their lives. Do not tell them to keep it all inside because I know it hurts, it feels like your heart is going to explode and you are going to die.

Since I was not allowed, I refrained myself from crying, staying alone so nobody can feel how sad I was. I felt so bad for my siblings that they had to go through all this and that if our mother was alive, this would have never happened.

I was already trying my best to keep myself together when I saw the woman, coming inside from the gate, saying she would take my sister and I with her. She had come back to pick us and take off with her. I don't know why, but I hated this woman thinking she was going to take us away from our father and family. I started thinking what if she actually took us away? I tried to appear in front of her as least as possible.

When everything was over, she went to my father and

said, *"I know you are young and I know you want to have a life, that is why I am here, I am going to take the two of your children with me."*

Hearing this, the others joined in saying, *"Okay, I will take the oldest one," "I will take the little boy."*

It was as if we were pieces of furniture or something and not human beings, like come on; we are not objects, we are humans, we have feelings, give us a break!

I can never forget how my father reacted to the situation. After hearing what everyone had to say, he said, *"No! Those are my children, and they are not going anywhere. They are going to stay with me. It doesn't matter how much I struggle; they will stay with me for as long as I live."*

I was so afraid of losing my father after I had to lose my mother, but thankfully, that didn't happen. I will always be grateful for this. My father was a great human being; he was so amazing that he just lost his wife yet decided to stay back with his four children.

My father worked in shifts. He used to work hard day and night, so he was hardly home and would come back very late. Now, it was just my older sister left to take care of us. My sister used to go to school in the morning, and we would be kind of left alone in the home.

Since my mother was not around anymore, I started going to school regularly. I met little girls of my age and made new friends. One day, a girl came to me and said, *"I don't think you care that your mother died because I never see you cry."*

Little did she know that I was told from home that I am not supposed to cry and bottle it all up inside. Therefore, whenever anyone talked about my mom, I used to remain silent.

The house we lived in was quite far from all our relatives. Once, my aunt said to my father that since he worked so much and was always away, she wanted us children to come live with her, where my mother used to be. Our father thought for a moment, then looked at us and said, *"Pack everything you want to take with you, including your clothes and toys. I will drop you all to your aunt's, and we'll talk about it later."*

While packing our things, I asked my older sister what was going on? Why were we leaving? What was going to happen to our beautiful home? And all she said was, *"I don't know, just do as our father told us to."*

Our father was a very strict and tough man, whatever he said, we had to do it. Any decision he made, we had to obey. We would never argue, and we had no choice either. We did not have our mother with us anymore, so we did not have anyone to run to; we had to listen to whatever our father said.

No matter how much we did not want to leave our home, we had to go to our aunt's house. I hoped that we got back to our own home as soon as our father was settled, and his workload lessened. I prayed for the happy days, but all my hope became vague when the next day, I saw a big truck coming to our aunt's house. The truck contained our beds, some furniture, and other belongings that we had left behind. I asked my father, *"What's going on?"* And he said, *"We are going to turn the house back to the bank, and we are going to live here in your aunt's house."*

The news hit me like a hammer; we had already lost our mother, now we have to lose our home and our freedom too. I didn't have my own bedroom. We were living in someone else's house. Could things get any worse?

You have to live through the worst parts of life, so you never take the best parts for granted.

They gave my older sister a separate bedroom. I had to sleep with my younger sister in another bedroom with one of my aunts, and my father and little brother stayed in one bedroom. Although my aunt had a nice and comfortable home, at the end of the day, it was not our own house, and we were not free to do anything. Going to my aunt's was traumatizing, and I believed it was the biggest mistake my father made, even though her and my father was just thinking about our safety since my father was always busy with work, and she did not want anything to happen to us.

I appreciate certain things about her as she taught me how to clean, how to do certain things that I didn't know how to do, but at the same time, I felt like I was being abused. I felt like we were taken advantage of, and every day was deliberately being made difficult for us.

My aunt used had us clean the house every Saturday, which was okay, but the way we were being treated was just not fair. We, my little sister and I, alone had to clean the entire house, which included three large bedrooms, a dining room, a living room, a kitchen, and a bathroom. Even though one of my aunts used to help, it was too much for us. I was only nine years old and my other sister eight years old

Besides, I had to go grocery shopping on my own, can you imagine?

I need people to realize that there is a God up there, watching over everything. He would justify every injustice. Therefore, even when someone is at your mercy, do not take advantage of that. When a child loses one of his parents, a lot of people try to take over their lives, but just because one doesn't have a mother does not mean they should be treated that way. It's unbelievable how people treat you when you don't have a mother.

My aunt used to smoke a lot, so every time she needed a cigarette, she would send me to buy one for her and I had to light it up for her, and if I said I didn't know how to do it or gave it to her without lighting it up, she used to yell at me. Therefore, I knew how to smoke since I was a child, I did not know how to inhale, but I had to put that cigarette in my mouth in order to light it up. I had to do it that way or else I am screwed. It was as if we were living a life of slaves, and we had no choice but to obey our aunt's orders.

Among all the chaos, the thing that hurt me the most was

what my younger brother had to go through. My aunt had two little boys who used to tease and abuse my younger brother. Whatever they said, my younger brother had to do it. All these things were happening behind my father's back, and we never had the courage to tell him. He had no clue what was happening to us, and we did not want him to know either. He was so protective about us that he would get really furious if he had the slightest of idea how we were being treated.

He could never see us in pain, and if anybody said anything wrong to us, he would get extremely angry. That is why we had to hide things from him. I never said anything to him because I did not want to upset him. I knew if I said anything to my father, we were going to be on the streets because we did not have a house anymore.

I know it wasn't just my mother who died, but that was my aunts' sister also. I understand my aunts were in pain too. I remember the day my mother died; my youngest aunt was devastated because my mother was everything to her. She was the nicest of all my aunts. She was also sharing the same roof with us. She was in her early 20s and would try to protect us in every possible way. Back in my country, in the neighborhood we lived in, the light used to go off, so when that happened, it was dull and boring. However, here, alongside with our youngest aunt, we used to play music, sing, go out, and play games. So, it wasn't always horrible, we had good times too.

Two years passed by, and life seemed to have gotten back on the track, but it was not going to stay on the track for long. My older sister was sixteen by then, and one morning she got really sick. She was continuously throwing up. I followed her to the bathroom and said, *"I don't know, but something's very wrong with you."*

I got so scared. All I could think about was she got sick exactly like my mom, and now I am going to lose her too. We got her checked, and it came as a shock to us when the doctor told us my sister was pregnant. Nobody could have ever imagined or even thought that this could be the reason she is throwing it all up. I couldn't believe it.

By the time we knew, she was already six months pregnant. She had hidden it from all of us because she was so scared of my father. She was scared of how he would react or how everyone else would react. She knew that nobody would ever see her the same way again, which kept her mouth shut. But no matter how much you hide; the truth always has its way out.

My sister was the oldest niece from both sides of the family. So, when everyone found out, they were obviously so angry at her.

My father was quite old fashioned; therefore, it came as a huge disappointment to him too. He was so hurt that he stopped talking to my sister. He told her, *"How dare you do things like that when you're supposed to be taking care of your brothers and sisters? I work so hard to give you guys the best of everything, and this is what you give me in return?"*

I could feel how painful it was for my father to know that my sister was going to be a mother at a very young age. I used to observe and wonder what would happen to my sister's life? She was still a child herself; how would she handle a little baby? I used to pay attention to everything that happened and would tell myself that I was not going to let this happen to me.

The time flew away in a blink of the eye, and my sister

gave birth to the baby. She struggled a lot even though she had support from the family and my father. The reason I am bringing this up here is that I want people to know that when you are young and witness such things, you think what I was thinking. Everything that happened had a massive impact on my life, and I can never forget any of it.

I remember the day my sister gave birth to the baby. Even though my father was not talking to my sister, he used to ask me how she was doing. That afternoon, he came home and asked me where is my sister and how she was doing. I told him that she went to the hospital and had the baby. The next moment I remember is he got dressed and rushed to the hospital to meet his daughter.

This is the thing about parents, no matter what mistake you made or how bad you were as a daughter or a son, they always forgive. Their hearts are made of wax, no matter what, they always melt to their children's happiness. That does not mean a child can do whatever the hell he/she wants to. We must respect the love and care our parents have for us. We should return the sacrifices they make for us and should never hide anything from them because, at the end of the day, it is nobody's but our loss. A lot of things happened throughout that time. Our family was against the baby and a single mother. They were more worried about what they were going to tell the people when they ask about it. There was so much going on within the family that we ended up leaving our aunt's house and went to our grandmother's house.

I was only twelve years old, watching my sister struggle at a very young age. We had no home to live in and had to move here and there with a baby. I was so young, but still, all that I had in my mind was the thought that I am not going to allow this to happen to me.

"Life is 10% what happens to you and 90% how you react to it."

-Charles R. Swindoll

The time went by, things got a little easier for my sister, but it sure taught her a lesson. She regretted so much that she used to tell my younger sister and me to always look at her as an example and never do what she did.

She used to tell us, it's *not about the child or having a family. I am very much happy that I have a son today, and I was able to give birth to him, but look at the struggle and humiliation that I am going through. This is why, never allow this to happen to you.*

Obviously, we both, my sister and I, knew what she was talking about. We were continuously struggling, and the worst part of it all was, we didn't have a place to live. In my head, I always used to wonder why we had to go through so much struggle. I couldn't understand because my father was not unemployed. He was making good money, so why couldn't we stay in our own home? Why did we have to struggle in other people's houses? At first our aunt's and now our grandmother's? Although I knew our father was just worried about our safety, I missed our old house. I missed my mom a lot because if she was alive, we wouldn't have to go through so much abasement.

All these things left a significant impact on my life but taught me a lesson at the same time. I used to say I would never put myself in such a situation and that I had to do great things in life. I used to encourage myself, saying, *"I know my future is going to be bright, and I am going to do a lot better than this."* Sometimes we wish improvement for ourselves. It's when we have a broken leg or a fractured arm or when we cannot see because we are blinded.

What we need to understand is that we still have a brain

working inside our heads. We should never let our physical abilities stop us from doing certain things. We should never allow our present situation to be eternal situations for us. Always strive for better days, and for that, we need to have the mentality that we have to pursue our dreams and have certain goals. Learn to set goals for yourselves, or else you will be lost.

I am saying this because I lost my mother, I lost my home, but I did not let it stop me from achieving my goals. I did not let what happened with my sister ruin the concept of parenthood. I learned from it. I used to tell myself that the day I become a parent, a mother, I would do everything to give my children the best life and never let them struggle. I remember my mother's words from the day before she passed away, she whispered in my ears, *I know you are going to be a great mother.* I always had that in my head.

I used to tell myself that I am going to work hard for my children. I want to be a role model, and I want them to look up to me as an inspiration. Just like for me, my father was my role model. He worked so hard to make ends meet when all the money was going into my mother's treatment. And even now he works hard so that we do not have to face any problems in our lives. He is my hero and the best father anyone can have. We started living at our grandmother's house, and I have to say it was beautiful there. We lived there with my uncle, my grandmother, and my grandfather. My grandfather was a criminal judge, and my grandmother was a college teacher while my uncle was a cardiologist. My father's side was quite educated, and therefore, I was surrounded by very well educated and professional people.

One thing I remember is that all of them, my uncle, my grandfather, and my grandmother, were dressed up nicely all the time. As of the side of my mom as well. I remember my grandmother was not home most of the time because of work; mostly, she used to be in the United States.

At my grandmother's house, everything was different. Although we used to do all the cleaning, go to school, and do everything like we used to back at our aunt's, we were happier here because we didn't have the pressure that we received from my aunt. We knew what we had to do; nobody commanded us anything. We knew that we had to help around the house and work. They also had a dog in the house that belonged to my uncle. He was a lovely dog. I used to play with him all day. We also used to sit and talk to our grandfather. He used to tell us so many stories about the history of the Dominican Republic and all the press dealings. Stories about himself when he used to be in court, how many people he used to arrest, and all the criminal cases that he handled. He would tell us all that, hoping one of us would become a lawyer or something. Listening to his stories always felt so pleasant and relaxing.

We had more freedom here, I didn't have to do all the things that I was doing at my aunt's house like lighting cigarettes for her, yet I was still lighting cigarettes, not for anyone but myself.

At my grandmother's house, I realized that I was craving for a cigarette. I sneaked out of the house and got myself a pack. You won't believe it, but I was only 13 years old when I started to smoke. Only because I used to light up a cigarette for my aunt, I didn't know how to inhale it, so I used to puff. I don't remember when I got used to it, but I had the taste in my mouth, and I used to smoke because my body was asking me to do it. I used to smoke hiding from everyone. Nobody knew about it, not even my sister I shared the room with. My father used to smoke, and in my head, I knew he would never want to know that his daughter smokes too, so I hide it from him. I had a pack of cigarettes with me all the time because I was kind of addicted, all thanks to my aunt. People don't realize the impact they leave on other people's lives with their actions. That is why we have to think like a human before we do something because you don't know what you're doing to a child's life, and you may never know what impact you are leaving on them.

As a child, because you are so young, you are afraid to even speak for yourself. You are scared of saying no because they know that you are not going to say anything to the person who is protecting you; in my case, my father. I knew my father's temperament, and I knew if my father found out, everything's going to turn into a painful tragedy.

Therefore, I had to keep my mouth shut. I was kind of getting blackmailed because my oldest sister and youngest aunt knew what I was doing, but they were quiet and didn't utter a word. They couldn't say anything, mainly because they didn't want anything bad to happen either. But at my grandmother's, it was different. I was lighting cigarettes for myself, and no one knew.

Although we were free here, we were strictly not allowed to go outside. That, too, because my grandfather was a criminal lawyer. We had friends who we used to talk to, but we were not allowed to go out to play with anyone. The friends we had were those from the school, so we only met them at school or sometimes would go to the grocery store and see them.

The house we lived in was much gated. Since my father was very protective of us, whenever he left for work, he used to lock the door from the outside and tell our grandfather not to let us go anywhere. We were locked in there for the rest of the day.

Despite that, I made very nice friends in that neighborhood. We were allowed to see them for a short time. My father never allowed us to sleep in someone else's house. He was like that because my sister had a baby at a very young age, and he wanted to protect myself and my little sister from going through the same. What he did not know was that I had already set my mind that I would never allow that to happen to myself. Sometimes you plan your future, but you never know what's going to happen next. Things can always turn against you, and sometimes we do not have any control over them. Whatever we say that we would never get into, can happen to us.

Life is full of surprises. Your fate can turn against you. Basically, life pushes you against your will. As much as you have your mind set that this is not going to happen to you, you lose control, and things happen otherwise. Therefore, I learned throughout my life that never believe in never, there is no such thing like never, because you don't know what is going to happen.

Don't ever say never because, despite the fact you have made your mind, you never know what life has in store for you.

Life is full of surprises. Not all these surprises are pleasant, so you need to be ready for what life brings you.

Chapter 3
From the Dominican
Republic to America

Do you know how it feels? Leaving your own house, the country you were born in, and moving into a completely different place? I am sure a lot of people experience this once in life, but their life afterward must not have been as difficult as it was for my family and myself.

It was summer when we decided to move to America from the Dominican Republic. I was 15 years old. One of my father's older sisters had sponsored us so we could come, live here, and have a better life. After getting the paperwork through, we would get a visa from immigration to go to the United States. But leaving my country was not easy. It was hard for too many reasons.

First of all, even though my mother was gone, I always felt she was there. I felt like her spirit was with me all the time. Therefore, moving out seemed like another detachment from my mother. It was as if I am saying good-bye to all the memories that I made with my mom. I was saying good-bye to my childhood, and that hit me hard. Besides that, my oldest sister couldn't bring her son with her, who was only two years old. We were leaving him behind, even though she was ready to bring him with us. The reason she couldn't bring her son with us was that when my aunt put the paper through, she told my father not to pull his information through immigration. She was afraid that my sister would have to stay back. She said after my sister was there, she would be able to do the paperwork to bring him too.

Both the reasons were weighing me down to stay back in my home country. I wanted the time to pause so that we remain there together forever. However, you don't always get what you desire. I didn't want to leave, but I had to. I felt like there was something I was leaving behind that was so important to me, and I wouldn't be able to have it again. It was as if I was leaving a part of myself behind, and I would never be the same again.

My father was not moving with us, even though he was coming with us right at the moment. He said he would come to the United States once he was done finishing some work here in the Dominican Republic. I told my father I would stay with him. Hence, my sisters and my little brother came to America. They went to Puerto Rico with my aunt to stay with her for a while. After losing my mother, I had to experience what it was like to live without my siblings. They all left. It was so heartbreaking and challenging for me to endure because that was the first time, we were separated from each other. It was tough, but deep down, I knew that we would live together again, and I was going to see them soon. Little did I know that life had a lot more lessons to teach me.

I didn't want to leave my father behind because I felt like I was already leaving so much behind, I don't want to leave him alone here. After my mother, I got very attached to him. I stayed back with him for another month in the Dominican Republic, while my siblings left to Puerto Rico, which was the country we needed to migrate to.

I don't know how, but that one month went so fast, and the time came for my father and me to move to America. I had a pleasant time with my father and my aunt back in Dominican. I am so thankful to my aunt for sponsoring us to move to the United States. Again, it was definitely not easy to abandon my friends and the country I belonged to. I had to leave so many of the things that were mine because I couldn't just bring everything with me. Nevertheless, there were a few things close to my heart that I brought with myself. When I was small, and my mother was alive, she used to make a lot of things out of art and crafts. She made this little pouch for me, which was like a little purse that I used to carry around the house because I was so happy that she had made it for me. I took it along with many other things she made for me. I felt like I brought pieces of my mother along that I could hold on to forever.

The day was finally here, and I was so happy that I am finally going to see my siblings because I missed them so much, and I had never been apart from them for so long. But the day my father and I immigrated to Puerto Rico, was the day my sister and my brother were moving to New York. I felt like crying when I got to know about it. I didn't even get to see them, but I still hoped to see them soon.

I can never forget how my older sister wrote a letter to me and left it under the pillow in the room in my aunt's house, where I was going to stay. The letter said *I am sorry I have to leave. I am going to miss you again. I am not going to be able to see you for now, but we will meet soon and other beautiful things…*

Back at that time, in 1992, we didn't have cellphones as we do now in order to communicate. To call each other from landline was just not appropriate since we were not in our own home but others'. She didn't want to bother them; therefore, she left this beautiful letter for me saying how much I mean to her, that everything is going to be okay, that they had a great time in my aunt's house, but they have to come to New York because that's where we were going to move eventually.

One important thing that I learned from my father was valuing togetherness. He always wanted to keep us together and stable. The irony is, if we go back to the beginning of my story, it's like ever since we lost our mother, we have been jumping from places to places in our efforts of getting to one place we could call ours. I always used to say that I wanted stability in my life and that I didn't want to be jumping around because I used to feel sad about us. I had this in my mind that when you don't have a mother, it's like your life is over. You can never have stability. Even though my father was always there for us to make sure we have that type of life that he always wanted for ourselves, we had no choice but to jump from one place to another.

My father and I were living in my aunt's house in Puerto Rico. A month went by, and my father and I finally moved to New York. That's when I reunited with my siblings.

We were in Brooklyn, but again, we didn't have a place to live. Like always, my sisters stayed in one of my aunt's house while I stayed in another aunt's house. My father went to his own sister's house with my brother. This is how we all united in New York, only to get separated again.

One of the reasons why my aunt wanted my father to immigrate to the United States was because she said that he would get a better job here. My father was a mechanical engineer, but unfortunately, he didn't get that opportunity and was working in a factory. It was so devastating to see my father step down from being the supervisor of a company to come here and do the job of ironing clothing. However, after a while, she was able to move from the factory and started working in a college doing maintenance. My father was very responsible and didn't let us know for a while what he had to do to support us.

Even though I didn't want to leave my country, I fell in love with New York from the moment I arrived here. I am the type of person that adapts to places and situations. I don't have a problem adjusting myself to any situation. I try to understand the environment and adjust myself accordingly. Maybe I have this in myself because I grew up adapting myself to places. Living with my aunt in Brooklyn was not easy. She had two daughters. One of them, I don't know what was happening to her, but I think she was grudging, I can't think of anything else, because I was close to her sister more.

I used to go to this park called Prospect Park in Brooklyn at night with my other cousin. It's such a beautiful park. No matter how hard I tried, I couldn't quit smoking. Even though I was so naïve and innocent that I thought people would never find out that I smoke, I knew that I smelled. My body, my clothes, my jacket, everything smelled of cigarettes.

It had only been three months since we got here, and one night, one of my cousins smelled the cigarettes in one of her jackets that I borrowed. She got so upset that she said she didn't want me in the house anymore. It was around 11 pm, and she wanted me to leave. I didn't know what to do.

My cousin went straight to my aunt (her mother) and told her that I had to leave. The reason why I'm talking about it here is that when we are young, sometimes we don't think about others and we do silly things. My cousin and I were almost the same age; I am six months older than her. I thought maybe she was a little bit spiteful because of my closeness with her sister, which is why she was overreacting. She put her mother in a tough situation, saying that she had to pick either her or me and that if I stayed there, she would leave. I remember I slept on the staircase that night.

My aunt had picked her daughter and told me I had to leave. The reason it hurts me when I talk about it is that when you are a grown-up, and you have a child, you are the owner of that place. You do not allow your child to make decisions, and my aunt, who I respect a lot, couldn't understand why her daughter was doing this.

I didn't call my father, but the next morning, I called my other aunt and told her what had happened. I was, of course, crying while narrating everything. She told me I could come to her house. Even though I knew she was out of space, I went to her house, where I used to sleep with my sisters in one little tiny bed. My older sister slept on the floor so we could sleep on the bed. It was a very difficult time for my family.

That's when I realized that you do not just lose your mother, you lose so many things with it. That is why I always used to say that the moment I became a mother, I would give endless love to my children. They would have the best mother in the world. I would sacrifice anything to make them happy and stable. Also, being a girl and going through so much in life, I never wished to have a daughter. I was traumatized. I felt that boys were stronger and could handle everything effortlessly. I finally called my father and explained to him what had happened. That's when he told me to come over, and we would find a solution. There was an empty apartment in the building he was living in with my aunt (his sister). It was a little studio apartment.

We were able to move to that studio. It had two bedrooms, a kitchen, and a small space, which was enough to pull four chairs. The bedroom that belonged to us was of pretty good size. Each of us sisters had a separate bed in the room. My father was in the other room with my younger brother.

It was way better if we compare it to the time we were living in our aunt's house where we had to be on the bed by 8 o'clock at night because we had to go through my aunt's bedroom to go to the room that was assigned to us. Her husband used to go to work, so we were simply not allowed to come out of that room before eight in the morning. It was kind of a curfew, but thankfully, we only had to live there for one month.

My aunt was a sweetheart and nice too. However, we had to follow her rules since we were living in her house. That one month felt like forever. I used to get to see my brother only at the weekends. Other than that, I only talked to my father and my brother over the phone. Even though we were going through so many things, I always used to smile. I never used to show my real feelings to anyone, and nobody had the slightest of an idea of how miserable I felt deep down.

The day my father found that apartment, we moved in together. We were all so happy to finally be together again. We were able to have our freedom. We were able to have our own place even though the neighborhood was not as great as the one we were living in before.

My father was young, in his early 40s, so he wanted to, of course, also enjoy his life.

We were so scared because the neighborhood was shady. My father was so strict with us that we were not allowed to be outside. We were never allowed to even stand in front of the building. We were only allowed to go from home to school. If we had to go to the supermarket, we would go there and come back home directly. We were not even allowed to talk to anybody - that was the life that we had.

I always felt kind of like claustrophobic, because my father didn't want us to do a lot of things, he was afraid of anything that could happen to us. He loved us and wanted to protect us. He always made sure that we had everything we ever needed. I remember when I first got my menstrual periods, I didn't have my mom to tell, so I had to tell my father. He was the one who bought feminine napkins for his three girls. We never went to the store to buy them. I didn't even know how to go to the store and ask for it. He took care of us like a mother.

So, the apartment we were moving to was on the second floor, and my father's sister used to live on the fifth floor. I didn't know my aunt much, so I started to get to know her slowly. Besides my aunt, a lot of my relatives from my mother's side used to live there as well. We had a great time there with my cousins, and life had started to look a lot better. My older sister started working, so she had to go to the office while my other siblings and I started going to school again. We were slowly getting back to our life.

After struggling for months from my mother getting sick to her funeral and jumping from houses to houses, we finally had an entire apartment to ourselves where we were in charge. We had a place to live together under one roof. It was as if the sun was finally coming out after a very long and dark night, the clouds were finally moving away, and brighter days were coming.

The rays of the sun shining down on us also gave us a message of freedom. We knew that this was our place. We could jump, we could scream, and nobody was going to say anything to us. We had a place that we could call our own. We were all together and finally stable.

Out of the darkness, only light can come, after a long lonely night, comes the sun...

Chapter 4
The Return of Gardner

It's the 'unexpected' that changes our lives...

We moved into our apartment, and finally, everything was beautiful again. After struggling for months, we got our freedom back. We were all so happy, realizing we had a place to live at last. It was kind of like a happy new beginning.

But happiness does not always last for long because life is never just about ups and ups. It is all about ups and downs. And after every up that we experience, we have to go down or else the roller coaster of life will never progress. And this time, it was an old enemy that was coming back to scare us to death and steal our happiness.

A few days after we moved in, my oldest sister started feeling a lot of pain in her mouth. She had no idea what it was. She initially thought it must be a regular toothache and took a painkiller for it. Days passed by, but the pain did not go away, and she started worrying then. She wondered whether it was the toothache or something terrible was going on because the pain that she was going through was becoming unbearable. Therefore, to find out the real cause behind why she was having so much pain, she finally decided to go to the dentist. Typically, when you go to the dentist, they do the routine checkups. They do the X-rays and check your mouth using different objects. When they did the X-ray on my oldest sister's mouth, they found out that she had a lot of tumors in her mouth.

The doctors were amazed and surprised to have a patient with this weird X-ray report. Therefore, they started asking a lot of questions. They asked if our parents were still alive. My oldest sister told them that our mother was no more and that she died of some condition that we do not really know because we were so young.

All we knew was that she was very sick. The doctor asked my sister, *"Do you have any siblings?"* she replied, *"Yes, I have two more sisters and one brother."* To which he said, *"I need to speak to your whole family, your father and your sisters, everyone needs to get themselves checked. The reason being the condition that you have is very rare. We only know about such conditions when we go to colleges and medical universities. They have only existed in books for us, and we never really experienced any patient with such a syndrome in real life. Therefore, to be on the safe side, I need to check everyone. The only thing that I can do for you right now is to give you painkillers."*

Besides that, the doctor recommended that my sister should go and see a doctor for the colon. My sister was clueless as to why she needed to get her colon checked, while it was her mouth that was hurting. The doctor explained that because she had a lot of tumors in her mouth, they suspect them to be in her colon as well. Therefore, she had to get herself examined.

My sister did not think it was something serious. She was very young at the time - only nineteen years old. She thought she was too young to have a condition so serious. However, she was worried about it at the back of her mind.

She came back home and told our siblings and me whatever the doctor said. Everyone got concerned. My sister said, *"I am not sure, but everybody has to go."* Then she called our father, and after telling him everything, she made the appointments. This was not something that should or could be delayed, so she set the appointments immediately.

Also, the painkillers never worked for her, but she kept praying and believing that it was nothing severe.

The day of the appointment came. We got to the doctor, and they did our x-rays. One by one, they told all my siblings that they had the same tumors in their jaw. I was nervously waiting for my turn because, by then, I was sure that I would have the same disease. Miraculously though, the doctors said that they did not find any tumor in my mouth. This one of the reason of multiples how I was blessed to be skipped.

I was the only one who did not have that rare mouth disease that caused the "syndrome." The doctors said, *"Even though you don't have that in your mouth, I want you to go and get your colon checked."* I agreed because, sometimes, in this type of syndrome, tumors bell-up in your body when you go through puberty.

When we left the hospital, everyone else also agreed to get themselves checked because this type of condition can be inherited; it can jump from generations. Fortunately, or maybe, unfortunately, on my mother's side of the family, she was the only one who had this disease. Her siblings did not inherit it. Therefore, either the whole family can have the condition, or it can jump. In my case, all my siblings had it, except me.

It was 'The Return of Gardener Syndrome" because this was precisely the time this disease came back after my mother died of it. It was also the time when I finally found out the name of the disease that my mother was suffering from. When my mother was suffering from this syndrome, I was only told that she was sick. Nobody ever told me what type of disease or syndrome she had.

It was so shocking to know that all my sisters and brother had that syndrome, and we were all so young. However, I never thought I'm blessed because I do not have the disease. Instead, I started doubting whether I belong to this family or not. I started thinking I was not the child of my mother and my father. When you are young, you can think of such stupid things. I also did. I could not stop thinking about why I did not get the disease.

When we came back home from the doctor's, I ran to my father and asked him, *"I am not your daughter, right? Why you never told me that I am not your child? I want to know who my real parents are."* Since I did not know about the condition, I did not understand why all my siblings had it, and I did not. I told him that they all were sick, and I was not; therefore, I was not his daughter. I made this logic that if I did not have the disease, I did not come from them. That's what I had in my mind, and I was so upset about it. I so hated it and wanted my father to tell me the truth. I did not want to talk to my siblings because I thought I was not related to them. I was not told that this disease was the reason my mother died, and it can jump generations. I questioned the whole family. I called my aunt everyone else to tell me the truth. I kept repeating that I did not belong to my family.

I started to believe that my family had probably picked me up from the street or the church. Everyone in the family thought I'd gone crazy. They told me I looked exactly like my grandmother. They raised eyebrows on saying how I could think I'm not one of them or not a part of this very family. They calmed me down and explained to me that it was not necessary for everyone in the family to get the disease. They told me I was abundantly blessed because I was not suffering from it.

Anyway, the treatments started. A day came when my sister had an appointment to get her colon checked since the disease is related to the colon. They checked her colon while she was under Colonoscopy, and they found out she was full of something called polyps. The doctor asked for surgery as soon as possible. My sister was resistant since she was young and scared, so she kept throwing a lot of questions and even questioned the diagnosis. The doctors were trying their best to convince her to have surgery. Just when they told her why she needed it, and she was almost convinced, our dentist called and asked us to hold the surgery. He said it was essential to first have her mouth surgery done as her jaw was full of tumors.

Soon, we were at the dentist's again. She got on the surgery, and they removed two tumors from her jaw. My sister had two tiny scars on her face below her jaw, but nobody could see them. After my sister had the surgery, they called back and said my brother and my younger sister had to get the same type of surgery. So, my younger sister also got the procedure done.

Back then, not everyone knew about it as the condition is sporadic. Only some specific doctors deal with this condition, and you had to go to these specialists to get it diagnosed and treated. They told my youngest sister where the tumor was located in her jaw before they did the surgery. Later, my brother when under surgery as well. Therefore, my two sisters and my brother have the same scar under their jaws. After all this, my older sister had to get her colon operated. She went to see the Gastroenterology doctor, and they said we needed to do a few tests and a colonoscopy and endoscopy. The colonoscopy confirmed that she had all those tumors in her colon called polyps, and to prevent the polyps from becoming cancerous, she needed to have a sub-total colostomy.

Before they performed the surgery, the doctors told us that because she had so many polyps in her colon, they had to remove a part of her colon. This was because when you have this type of condition, the odds of polyps turning into cancerous ones are high. To prevent cancer, they had to remove part of the colon or almost everything. Such patients then get a colostomy bag to for survival.

My sister was not thinking about her future. She did not tell the doctors that it was fine, and they could do anything that needed to be done. She told them, *"Do whatever you want to do, but if I wake up with a bag in my stomach area or the opening area, I will kill you. You can only remove a part of my colon, and I am not signing for anything else."*

They performed the surgery on my sister. She spent a week or more in the hospital and then came back home. Everything was normal. Even though our mother died of this condition, we were not thinking that this condition is going to kill anyone of us because we were getting the right treatment. It killed our mother because the doctors did not give her the right treatment. Little did we know this is not how it works.

After my older sister was getting back on the track of life, my younger sister and brother had to go and get the colonoscopy done.

The test confirmed that my younger sister and brother had the same problem. The doctors had to remove a part of their colon, too. But they could not remove all the polyps in there. Every year, my younger sister and my brother would go to the doctor to get their polyps removed. But it was a tiring process. After all, who likes going to get surgeries done and that too, every year? In such cases, you eventually have to get your colon removed because polyps can become cancer.

Sometimes you think that life is perfect. You walk around the town beautifully dressed up with people complimenting you, without a slightest of an idea what life has in store for you. You never know what is going on inside your body. You do not show any signs because this condition is not visible and is inside of you. People never really realize or find out because you do not show. And you do not show it because you do not know it either. Nobody understands or even knows what you are going through. That is why I always say, *"Do not judge a book by its cover."* You may look beautiful outside, but nobody knows what you are holding inside or what you are going through in life.

Regardless, you have to keep your head up always. You do not need to let everyone know about your problems because not all of them respond as your family does. Not all of them understand. Some people feel sorry for you, some show sympathy, and some simply do not care.

For us, growing up with this condition was very hard. We wanted to keep it discreet. Not all our friends knew that everyone in my family was sick. We kept our pain to ourselves.

Imagine you are nineteen years old, and you discover you have a lethal disease. You have a child, you are young, you want to live and enjoy life, you want to do so many things, but you cannot because you have a deadly disease. Knowing that your siblings are going through such a condition just leaves you in so much pain. Even if you try to be happy, you cannot be. Just the thought of living with this condition for the rest of our lives was scary. We could not help but think about our mother that how she must have gone through so much pain yet never complained. She kept her pain to herself and proved herself as an epitome of patience, love, and care that she had for us. We missed our mother even more at this time, and I wished I could hold her in my arms for one last time and tell her that I understand her pain a lot better now. I wanted to say sorry to her for not being able to help her in any way. But I could not.

By this time, I was devastated. The last time I had felt this way was when my mother passed away. I was too naive when she passed away and too young, but that was not the case this time around. I was much more mature. I had developed the ability to feel everything so deeply, and believe me, I did.

Looking at my family suffer saddened me, but I felt left out. Although I kept reminding myself that *I am blessed to have skipped*, deep down, I wished I had the same disease. I did not want to be the one who consoles everyone and takes care of everything, but I had no other choice. Life had already taught me the lessons I never wanted to learn. I was mentally older than my actual age. I understood their pain, and I knew I was the only one to help them feel better. It was a huge responsibility, but I always reminded myself of how my mother would have wanted me to react or behave in such a situation. This gave me the strength to tackle things and kept me going somehow.

I knew that my sister and brothers were in a lot of pain. I felt their pain in every vein of my body. It hurt me to the core. It was not one or two members of my family who is going through this pain; it was all of them except my father. It broke my heart and kept me from being able to help my siblings, regardless of how badly I wanted to. The people in your family are the ones who support you in times of need, but there was no one except me to tell them all that they are going to be alright. I had to gather all the strength left inside my body to keep myself from smashing to smithereens. This was not the time for me to be weak; I had to be strong.

It was hard. It will be not if I say it was the toughest thing I ever encountered in my life. There were moments when my siblings got angry and upset. They said things to me out of anger, but all I could do is watch them suffer. I had to be patient enough to understand that they are only talking out of frustration. I could only imagine the pain they were going through and the condition that was making them weak with each passing day. I was shattered, and I used to cry myself to sleep. I missed my mother a lot. I wished she was here so I could feel a little less lonely. I could not help but think about how much I wanted to be able to help my mother, but I could not. Will I have to lose my siblings, too? I was unaware. The history was repeating itself, and I was once again terrified of what will happen next.

Even though I did not have the condition, I suffered equally. Honestly, the way I see it, my suffering was even worst. The reason behind it is that I was suffering seeing them suffer, was all alone, and that I was helpless. It was as if I am carrying the entire world on my shoulders. I was thinking inside my head that my siblings were each going through their own pain only. All they had to worry about was themselves, but that was not the case with me. I had to worry about all of them in addition to fulfilling all other responsibilities.

Nonetheless, I was really worried about all of them. I tried to keep myself strong and be there for them always. I tried my best not to let my weak side take over the situation. I decided that I will not leave them alone, no matter what.

Therefore, I used to skip school.

I stayed home and helped my elder sister to get through the day because her condition was getting worse. Simultaneously, to be able to help her better, I started studying about "the monster" – that Gardner Syndrome. I told myself that it is okay if I do not have this condition and that I have to help my brother and sisters in any possible way. That is what propelled me to learn about this syndrome.

I visited the doctors regularly with my sister and kept researching simultaneously. What I learned from my research and doctor visits is that Gardner Syndrome is a disease that is inherited from either of the parents, if they have it. If one of the parents has this condition, there is a 50/50 chance of the child getting the condition as well. In our case, my mother had the disease which was inherited to us. Fortunately, or unfortunately, all my siblings got the condition, except me. The average life-span of surviving with this disease is 45 years, and this was the scariest fact that I came across.

For me, life only meant suffering. There was no such thing as happy days, only better days, which were the ones in which we did not have to face any bigger issues. The minor ones were now part and parcel in our lives, though. They always remained. My mother suffered, and now my siblings were suffering. With this syndrome, you only suffer because you have to remove your colon. Your body can develop tumors called osteoma and desmoid. The desmoid is the tumor that grows in the abdominal part of your body. It can invade your organs, including your stomach, column, colon, liver, and kidneys. What's worse is that it only grows larger with time.

My elder sister suffered so much because of the desmoid tumor. Slowly, these tumors turned into cancer, and by the age of twenty-five, she was declared a cancer patient.

My sister's life before cancer was beautiful. She herself was a beautiful soul. Everyone loved the positive vibes she generated everywhere she went, and so, everyone loved her. Besides the positivity bit, my sister was a very self-sufficient and responsible woman. To her, life was exactly the way you look at it. You either suffer or learn to be happy with whatever comes your way. She loved her little son to the core, and he was enough for her to live all by herself for the rest of her life.

Nonetheless, she became very depressed because of the sickness and all those trying times she was going through. She was young and wanted to do so many things with her life, but she lost the hope of being able to do them ever. It was tough for her to give up on her dreams. This was the reason she was resistant to do so many things. One thing she dreaded the most was chemotherapy, which was because she was afraid that she was going to lose all her hair.

She was so young and beautiful, and of course, she did not want to lose her hair. No one would want that. At times, I used to ignore this. The rest of the time, I convinced her saying chemotherapy is the best thing to do because it could help her get better. However, the decision was all on her. I could not force her into anything, and in the end, she decided not to go for chemo and rely on medications only.

Every day was becoming harder for my oldest sister than the previous one. When she found out what she was suffering from, she was still working. She kept on working until she just could not. The condition was not as bad in the beginning as it got after developing cancer of course.. That is when she became disabled and struggled to fulfill her responsibilities. Therefore, she quit her job.

Her body was transforming, and, of course, not into something better. She got so sick that she was confined to bed. She could barely walk. It was heartbreaking to see what she was going through, but again, I could not do anything. Gradually, her body was becoming weaker and weaker. She was unable to do so many things, due to which she got into depression. She would not sleep and keep asking me if things will ever get better. Sadly, all I could do was stare at her face blankly until I could gather myself back together and give her some hope even though I was not entirely hopeful myself.

With Gardner's Syndrome, most of the tumors that grow inside your body are not cancerous. However, in my sister's case, they did turn into cancer. Like I said before, it depends on your body and genes. In her case, she had it in her genes, so the disease itself was very aggressive. My sister first developed a tumor in her face as mentioned before, below her knee, which is a very aggressive cancer tumor called sarcoma. Eventually, she had cancer spread in her body completely. It really bad with the time, and they finally had to remove the tumor that she had dent inside her leg. The monster was tough to control. Even after one tumor was removed, she had other tumors scattered in her body. You could even feel all those tumors in her hand and all over her skull. She had thick hair, but you could still feel them upon touching her skull. I never showed to her that I could feel them. I told her that there is nothing and she will be alright. Nevertheless, she very well knew what was happening inside her body.

The transformation of her body was crazy. The tumor in her stomach got so big that it started to show up on her skin. The next thing we know is, it broke her skin and started to pop out. It pressed all the veins inside her stomach. Such tumors invade so much of her abdomen. The abdomen is like the hub of it. My sister's legs had swelled up and gotten bigger than the actual size, which made it all the more difficult for her to walk. By this time, she could not walk. All the nerves inside her legs were pressed against each other.

The tumor in her abdomen grew so much that her back turned into a huge hump. She was five feet and six inches tall, but due to the hump, she looked shorter because she could not stand up straight. The pain of trying to put herself in a straight position was so unbearable that she gave up on walking straight at all. She had to shrink herself down to walk, and this made her look so small. Watching her walk like that was painful, and it brought so many memories back. It reminded me of my mother.

It was unbelievable how all of this was happening to us AGAIN. It was like we were living in a nightmare. It was as if the dark clouds were floating over our heads, and they would not leave until every inch of life was sucked out of our bodies. Everything was so horrible that I sometimes used to ask myself, "Is this a curse?" You know, in such a situation, you think of all the craziest stuff in your head. Even when you know the reality, it is hard to accept.

Nonetheless, my sister got sicker and sicker with each passing day lot of hospitalizations. We used to go to the hospital every day to be there with her. Trust me when I say, none of the visits gave us any hope. Since I was bound to home and hospitals, I could not go to school. I used to miss my classes because I did not want to be away from my sister. I was always close to her. I could not concentrate in school even if I went. No one was there. All my siblings were sick.

Although I had many friends in school and we used to enjoy ourselves and have a good time, I could not show up at school and I never really wanted to. I was scared and weak, but I never wanted the world to know about it.

Life brings us into many circumstances. In 1993, we moved again into our aunt's house. She had bought a beautiful home, which was a two-family house. My aunt called my father and asked him if he wanted to live on the second floor, which was more comfortable than our apartment back then. It was a full apartment with a kitchen, three bedrooms, and a living room. Therefore, my father said yes without delay. Again, we moved to our aunt's house in Brooklyn, New York, in a lovely neighborhood.

It was not difficult to move this time because we were going to have a better house, a better community. We were also going to have our aunt on the first floor, so it sounded good to us. We were no longer alone.

Not boasting, but I have to say that I am dexterous and strong-willed. I would not give up on anything easily. I kept learning about the disease my siblings were suffering from and grew up on my own while looking after them. I stayed strong all this while. Our dad always taught us to keep our head up and never let our crowns fall. He told us not to show anyone when we are weak, and that no matter what we go through, we have to be strong. *"Whining or smiling, you have to live your life through. So, why not just smile and endure than whine and make it more miserable?"* My dad said.

These were the words that I always had in my head and lived by. I learned that even if we have to live our lives struggling, we have got to live it. We should not give up until the end. You must keep fighting until you do not reach the 'end.' There will be times when we have to fight for our lives. After all, we are given this life to live and fight, not to give up as cowards do. This world is a battlefield, and you are a soldier on it. You have to keep fighting no matter how many times you are attacked or from what directions. You can either live as a conqueror or die as a loser. Do not throw yourself down. Keep on going until it is the end. That is what I did and grew up doing. That is my struggle, and that is how Gardner's syndrome changed the lives of everyone in my life. But what is really Gardner Syndrome?

Gardner syndrome is a form of familial adenomatous polyposis (FAP) that is characterized by multiple colorectal polyps and various types of tumors, both benign (noncancerous) and malignant (cancerous). People affected by Gardner syndrome have a high risk of developing colorectal cancer at an early age. The syndrome was first described in 1951. There is no cure at this time, and in its more advanced forms, it is considered a terminal diagnosis with a life expectancy of 35–45 years; treatments are surgery and palliative care, although some chemotherapy has been tried with limited success.

Even though the disease kept ruining our lives bit by bit, we continued fighting. My brother and youngest sisters are very strong, and I admired their courage. They did not give up. Despite the fact that my oldest sister was struggling to survive, bearing with the series of painful treatments, and spending most of her time at the hospital, she never gave up. She never got good news at any of her appointments, but she always had a hope that something magical was going to happen. She was exactly like our mother, never wanting to give up and showing everyone that she is strong. Deep down, all of us knew she was suffering badly, and that life had become a living hell for her.

None of it could topple her courage down, though.

I did not stop studying this condition. I learned so much

about Gardener's syndrome that I wished to create awareness for it. I teach people about it because it is such a horrible disease, it is like a monster that haunts you for the rest of your life, and I want to teach people how to defeat this monster, but in reality I just want to tell others who are suffering about this condition to be strong. Meanwhile, I want you, and whoever reads this, to remember this:

'The struggle never ends until life ends. And it should not even.'

Chapter 5
School Life

I knew from the early years of life that living in this world is never going to be easy. Everyone has to go through many ups and downs in life. There are times when we have to walk on the thorns to finally get roses. I lost my mother, and now my entire family was sick. I was not strong enough to bear another downfall. I had become very sensitive and impatient at that point in life, but I had the courage of my mother to endure everything life throws at me.

In the wake of all these problems, I was also not doing very well in school. Nonetheless, every phase in life has its share of bumps. I made great memories in school. Those moments I will never forget, and whatever I learned then will stay with me forever. I made new friends and have had delightful moments with them. We used to party hard, and this was something I was never expecting.

First of all, I was not in the country for long, so I did not know how to speak English. When I started going to High School in Brooklyn in 1992, I was placed in a bilingual class alone with my youngest sister. I believe that made it harder for me to learn the language. However, I always had in my mind that I have to learn English and never gave up on that. I wanted to make my father and my elder sister proud, so I was trying my best.

During my high school years, a lot of things were happening to me, all at once. Having my older sister sick was a big challenge for me. I had a hard time concentrating in school. I wanted to be there for her and accompany her to all her medical appointments, and I would. All her appointments were in the morning, due to which I missed a lot of my classes in school.

Although my older sister wanted me to concentrate on school only and not to miss my classes, I would not listen to her. I wanted to be there for her and go on her hospital visits, just like I accompanied mom. It was as if I was reliving those days. I used to feel my mom smiling at me while lying on the hospital bed, but it was in my elder sister. Although deep down, I used to pray that whatever happened with my mother, never happens with my sister, all of it felt just the same.

I would miss my classes and accompany my sister because I was so anxious to know what was going on with her. Also, I wanted to be there standing strong with my family during this difficult time that we were all facing. I used to say to myself, 'I need to be in school or else, how would I ever be able to learn English?' However, the thought that I needed to be there with my sister always won over.

The language barriers did not stop me from going to the doctors with my sister. In fact, going on medical appointments with my sister also contributed to my progress in learning the language somehow. Her doctors did not speak any Spanish, so I had to speak a little bit of English with them that I knew. It was quite helpful. It helped me improve my vocabulary, but there was much more left to learn.

In case you are wondering why I was so hard on myself for learning the language, there were many reasons behind it. The biggest reason of all was that I wanted to shut several mouths, especially a girl at school who used to make fun of me. Yes, I was bullied at school by a young blonde girl for not being able to speak English. She was of the same age as mine. We were both 16-year-olds at the time.

I do not understand till date why, but the forward would not miss a single chance to bully me. She would not only bully me but also harass me and shout so many things like, "You don't know how to speak English? From where do you get money to dress so nicely?" and all the other crazy things that you can imagine. She did so every single day.

Regardless of whether I was in the gym, wandering around, or in the locker room, if she even found me passing by anyplace, she bullied me. I think she considered it her responsibility to insult me. She would always say, "Hey, Stupid! You don't know how to speak English." It was getting out of hands, and a point came when my physical health started to get affected. I started considering myself as a dumb person who did not know basic shit. With time, all this torture took the shape of anxiety and stress.

The incidents kept repeating, and it went on for weeks until one day when I could no longer take it. I told my younger sister that I was going to fight the girl at the school's cafeteria when the lunch break was over. I still recall that day, I was very quietly sitting at the school cafeteria with my head down, and she kept approaching me with her remark. I ignored her and remained silent, pretending to ignore her comments. As soon as the bell rang, the bully girl started walking towards the exit. Right then, I got off my seat and walked towards her with rage. My younger sister was so concerned about me because she was afraid that something terrible was going to happen to me. She was begging me not to create a scene and just let it go, but I was done bearing. Now, there was no going back. I did not care what happens with me next because, at that very point, I was boiling with anger. I wanted to put a stop to this blonde girl's bullying.

I thought fighting her was the only solution because I was not able to speak English fluently enough to let her know how I felt about her behavior towards me. I wanted to let her know how much words can hurt, so I had no choice but to fight. When words do not work, you have to get up and fight for yourself. That is what I was doing. I proceeded to walk towards her. When she was almost by the exit, I screamed her name. She turned around, and I punched her in the face. That is how the fight began, and I also recall this girl was taller than me, but believe me, I did not care and kept fighting. We fought so badly, and the crowd was screaming our names aloud. Nonetheless, I only concentrated on hitting her as hard as I could. My sister was continuously trying to pull me away from her but failed badly. I just fought with her like I was nuts. It felt like there will never be another chance to take my revenge. We kept fighting like crazy. It was so bad that the school security guard came inside to resolve the fight. When even he could not pull me off from her, he called more guards to help. I guess I was so tired and mad about holding everything inside for so long that I did not know how to stop myself from hitting her. I still do not know what had gotten into me.

Finally, with more guards, they were able to pull us apart while I ended up on the floor, I was kicking her so fast that at one point my legs were just kicking in the air. They got us off, and my sister, the girl and I were taken to the principal's office. We were suspended for about two weeks.

After the decisions, we were sent home. The bully girl, however, was still filled with bitterness. She called her boyfriend and other guys to have another fight. Guess what? We did have another fight on the street. One of the guys was holding my sister, so she does not interfere in the fight. The girl was going to scratch my face with her long nails, but I grabbed her hands from my mouth so badly that it started to bleed. To compel me to let go of her hands, her boyfriend started to smack my face, and believe me, it was hard. Nevertheless, I did not feel anything, which I guess was because my body was so hot with rage. I felt numb.

Finally, the fight was over with no winners or losers. They all just went home and left my sister and me alone. I remember that night I was so afraid to let my father know what happened in school and on the street. Sadly, I did not have any choice because I ended up in the hospital with a lot of pain in one of my legs. The pain was so severe that I could not walk. The doctors told my dad that I had disjointed my right leg.

So, the time was here, and I had no choice but to tell my dad what had happened at school. I had to tell him how I ended up with a disjointed leg, and why was I suspended for two weeks. Surprisingly, dad did not say anything and was not upset with me at all. I guess he understood my situation, and he would have done the same if he was in my shoes.

Two weeks passed by. My sister and I went back to school. The blonde girl was not allowed to be close to me and vice versa. The timing of our lunch breaks was changed; therefore, we never really saw each other. She never messed around with me again, or you can say, she did not dare to.

Sometimes we have to do whatever we have to do to put an end to certain situations. I did what I felt was right, and trust me, I do not regret a bit of it. I was relieved that she had learned her lesson. Everything seemed to be back to normal. I made a new group of friends. They were nice, but all they wanted to do was cut classes and hang out. Of course, I was happy with my friends and hanging out everywhere with them in front of the school, in the school hallways, and going to "HOOKIE PARTIES." It was all a lot of fun, and I loved my new friends dearly. They made me feel a lot better about myself.

One day, I was randomly invited to another hooky party, where I met a guy. We started to dance, and our talks never ended that day. We kind of clicked with each other instantly, and to my surprise, we were going to the same school.

Days passed by, and we continued to see each other even more frequently. I did not stop the bad behavior of cutting classes. The only difference was that now I was skipping classes to see my boyfriend. We had loads of fun together. For a while, I completely forgot about all the stress and anxiety I was going through.

Nonetheless, everything in life comes with consequences. Since I was continually skipping classes, one day, my father was called from the school, and guess who called him? It was the principal himself. He explained to my father that I was not doing well in school. He said it was not only about me, but my younger sister was also not present in most of the classes. That was because I used to take her with me. He was told if this continues, we were going to get kicked out of the school. Of course, my father was very upset with us. I remember we had a very serious talk that night after a long time.

When we are young, we do not realize all these crazy things that we do just to have fun. As time passes and the blindfold falls off, we realize that the reality is way more horrible. That time was great. Some parents do not realize that keeping your child under so many restrictions does not help with anything. In fact, it makes them even more curious about what it is that our parents are stopping us from. In my case, my father did not give me a certain freedom. Freedom that I should have been given as a right. Not to excuse myself for my behavior, but at the time, I just wanted to have fun and never thought of the consequence this behavior will put me through. After the complaint at home, we stopped cutting classes for a while. However, we could not just get rid of the habit completely. We started at it again after some time. The school set up another meeting with my dad, and we were given a second chance with the final warning. You know you can stop someone from doing certain things, but you can never enforce your decision on them. I have learned this the hard way that children are meant to be dealt in a certain way. They must be taken care of, especially the ones who lose their mother. It is the responsibility of the elders not to be very strict or harsh and think rationally. Sometimes, we, as teenagers or young adults, do not want to listen to our parents.

We just want to do whatever we want to. We make mistakes, and the consequence only hurts us. The process might be difficult, but it helps us learn to distinguish between good and evil on our own. So, it is better to let your children make mistakes and learn rather than enforcing restrictions on them. Just let them blossom slowly like a flower. They are sensitive and may break if dealt with roughly. It is a very critical procedure, and you have to be very careful with every move you make.

Chapter 6
Young Love

I believe, at every stage of life, the definition of love changes. It never stays the same, and people never really understand what it actually means. Young love has a certain charm and beauty. As we grow up, we begin to love all relationships around us differently, and it further keeps evolving with time. Over time, the definition of falling in love changes as well.

As a teenager, we have many crushes. We fall into believing all those crushes are love when we are experiencing them when in actuality, they are not. We do stupid things, end up in silly situations, and start thinking that life is tough. However, as we grow up and life unveils its bitter realities on us, we feel that we were better off being kids - carefree and without these burdens of life.

As a teen, most of what we think as love is merely infatuation or attraction. It is a part of growing up and learning. It makes life interesting and fun. At least that is how we feel when we are still there. We like receiving attention from the opposite gender, and that is where things go wrong. We think that we need the opposite gender to validate our beauty or prettiness, which I think this is why we need to teach our children from the very start that they are beautiful anyway.

My older sister had already faced the consequences of young love. I had learned my lessons from her, and I knew how to deal with guys. Little did I know I had much more to learn. My teenage years were great. I met this guy who completely changed my life. Among all the chaos and darkness that I had in my life, he was the only light of happiness and hope I saw.

He filled colors in my black and white world. I used to be so worried about my older sister and my siblings at home, but whenever I met him, I forgot about everything. All the worries of life vanished the moment I saw his face. Even though the feeling lasted for a while, it was always there and made me feel good. I was very happy with him, and so was he. Life seemed a little better with him. My perspective of looking at things was changing with time. I was so sure about him that I even told my dad that I was seeing this guy. I never told my father about any of my male friends. Of course, he told me to bring him over to meet everyone, so I did. He came to our house and met my father, and truth be told, my father was not happy with my choice. Obviously, though, this could not change my feelings towards him. My father knew that I liked him, so he just told me to be careful. He advised me to think about every step I take and look at all the perspectives before making any decision.

A few days later, my boyfriend took me to his home so I could meet his family too. I was on cloud nine. It made me feel I was important to him and that he was serious about me. It was a very sweet and romantic relationship. The kind of relationship you dream about as a teen. My life was complete. He was the first guy that I brought home to meet my dad. I was 16 years and was to turn 17 in a few months. We were both the same age. It was an ideal relationship for me at that time. We were getting more involved in each other with every passing day.

We used to see each other every day because we went to the same school. We were inseparable. I recall we did not have any class together, but we used to have lunch breaks at the same time. It was like I was living a perfect love story. We used to dress alike, wear the same shoes, shirts, pants, etc. If nothing else, we used to wear the same color and look like twins. This is how months flew away with him, and we were dating for a while now. We went to parties together, shopped together, and ate out. It was so much fun. He was very popular in school, which I think was because he was very outgoing. While he was already good looking, this quality made him all the more attractive.

One day I was in my regular class. When I came out of my class to go to the restroom, I passed by the hallway when I found him talking to a girl. I did not say anything at the moment and silently went away. I thought maybe she was his class fellow, and they were discussing something related to work.

However, rumors started to spread that they had something more than friendship.

A scandal was made, and everyone was gossiping that he was dating another girl. Oh my God, I went crazy. I wanted to punch everyone who talked shit in their faces, but most of all, I wanted to kick the shit out of him. My blood was boiling with rage. I immediately went to him and confronted him. He admitted at the time that he was. I felt like the ground was slipping under my feet. I felt deceived for the first time in life. My heart was broken, and I was in pain because I liked him a lot. Lots of commotion started to happen. He promised me he would not do it again, and I forgave him. That is all I wanted to hear and all I wanted - to get back with him. I did not want the good days to end so soon. I had gotten them after a lot of struggle. We continued with our relationship and forgot whatever happened with time. Everything was beautiful again.

The only thing that I did not like about him was this guy was very much possessive and jealous. He wanted to control everything about me, the way I dressed, the way I dance, even the way I walked, etc. Nonetheless, all of it did not bother me at the time because I thought it was okay for your boyfriend to be possessive and protective of you.

We spent most of the holidays together, attended each other's family functions, and no matter what went on in our lives, we were always together. Everything seemed stable for one more time. Life started to look like a bed of roses. At this point, we were together for more than a year. I thought everything was going well between us, and I was grateful for every moment.

Life has a funny but annoying way of telling it is not easy when you begin to think it is good. The same happened to me. Whenever I felt things were fine, life happened. All of a sudden, my boyfriend started to change. I don't know what had gone wrong or why he was behaving that way, but he was changing for sure. I started to wonder maybe he is seeing another girl, but I used to ask myself how he could see another girl when he was with me the whole time? These thoughts always made me feel stupid for feeling that way.

He started doing strange things. He was going to his home earlier to sleep practically, which was very unusual. I kind of ignored the situation and thought to myself that maybe he actually was tired. His behavior was very strange, though. I could not resist and asked him about what was going on. Of course, he denied and made excuses.

Things started to get out of hands. I became very aggressive with him and possessive about his whereabouts. His mother used to call me and tell me if he was going out. However, he used to deny every single thing. I used to cry so much because I did not want to lose my boyfriend, who I loved dearly. I was watching all my dreams shatter in front of my eyes.

I used to ask him and myself that what did I do wrong to deserve this. The only possible thing I could think of was maybe because my father was very strict and I could not, or you can say I 'was' not allowed to go out during the night, to the clubs, or late-night parties. I remember I went to the club with him one night and I wanted to dance my heart out, but I could not dance that much just because he was so jealous of me dancing. I did not have the freedom like other teenagers of my age during that time. I thought maybe that was the reason why he was changing and behaving so differently to me.

I always used to talk to my older sister about everything, and she always used to remind me to look at her as a mirror, meaning not to repeat the same mistake she made when she was a teenager. I always had that in the back of my mind. Nothing lasts forever, and I knew that very well ever since my mother passed away. I eventually found out he was going out with another girl. I confronted him. I recall that day very well. I was crying so much, asking him to tell me the truth, but he still denied it. Things were never the same again. We did not see each other much like we used to do; there were always excuses. I was so done with everything that one day

I went to him and said, *"Listen, I know who the girl you are seeing is, where she lives and everything about her."* That is when he finally admitted that he was going out with her. I could not believe what I heard. I was devastated. I felt like the sky had broken into millions of pieces and fallen on me, all at once.

When I asked him why he cheated on me, he said that he wanted to enjoy his life differently, and I was not prepared for it at all. At that point, I told him clearly that we cannot be together anymore, but he proposed to me again and told me to accept the proposal as proof of love. Wow!

This was unbelievable; first, you cheat on your girlfriend with another girl, and then you ask her to prove her love to you. When we are young, we are put into so many difficult and strange situations. In my case, what do you think I did? I loved this guy so much that I did not want to lose him at any cost. We had countless beautiful memories together. We used to talk about our future, creating a family and having children and so many of such cute relationship-things. But guess what? I decided to end this relationship once and for all.

I remember I was very much afraid of having sex and becoming pregnant. We broke up right then. I still remember that day we both cried so much. I did not understand why he was crying when he had another girl in his life already. I used to ask myself at that time if he really cared about me or if he ever loved me. I thought about the feelings he had for me, if any, and if he loved me as much as I loved him. I guessed not. He could have given me time if he did love me, but no, only sex was his priority.

We kissed for the last time, and before we said good-bye to each other, I remember telling him that, "*Look at me very closely because you probably won't see me ever again.*" That is how things ended with him. It was so painful that it can never be described in words. You know when you are young, you love too deeply and passionately. It was a very intense situation for both of us, but it was the only choice we had.

However, a week passed by, and his mother called me for something. She asked me to come over to her house, and the first thing I asked her was, *"Is he going to be there?"* and she replied, *"No, he is working."* She knew I would not come if he is there. I gave it a thought and then decided to go and see his mother. When I arrived at his place, he was there. I learned afterward that he asked his mother to call me because he wanted to see me again. Again, we cried so much, and I told him this would be the last time you are seeing me. I told him to think of me as dead because he would never see or hear from me again.

After all, my father got a call again from school, and this time, it was a final notice that my sister and I were going to be transferred to another school. Well, you probably must be asking yourself the same thing that I wondered back then. I did ask myself during that time that even if we get shifted to another school, at the time, who cared! My father was so disappointed with my sister and me. We got a list of different high schools to go to, so we began the search. As soon as we found another school, we got transferred.

Perfect timing it was. That is when I started to believe the popular phrase "that everything happens at the right moment and at the right time". It was so hard for me to get over him while getting to see him every day at school. I got very depressed and started cursing myself and my life. I never wanted to see him again. When we got the call for transfer, I thought, 'Wow! This is perfect. But this was not the solution.' I started overthinking. I thought to myself that everything that I had or loved, I lost. I started to drink nonstop. I was inebriated almost every day. Once I locked myself in the closet and cried until I did not have any tears left to cry. My father was not aware of it, but when I told him, he was happy that I broke up with him.

I was so mad at my father for what he said when he got to know. He asked me to sit down at the kitchen table, and he told me, *"Be happy that it happened now. You are still young and only 18 years old."* He was trying to make me feel better about everything. *"You are such a beautiful young girl; you could find somebody else. Don't forget it was his loss, not yours."* I did not care what my father said to me. Even though it was beautiful, I did not like those words. I was in so much pain that I did not want to hear anything.

The new school that I was transferred to had night classes as well. I was able to drink all day and attend school at night. Sometimes, I went to school half-drunk. I got so sick that I ended up getting hospitalized. I remember my older sister wanted to call the guy and let him know what was happening to me. I recall telling her while lying in the hospital, *"Don't you dare do that!"* She was so worried about me that she thought something bad was going to happen to me. I told her,

"He does not need to know anything about me. He is very happy with his girlfriend; do not disturb him." I remember all of it like it just happened yesterday. My older sister told me, *"So you don't really love him? If you do love him, you will not let him go."* My reply to her was, *"I love myself more than anyone. I will make it through all of this, just give me some time to heal."*

I was severely depressed, and it was hard for me to escape it, but thank goodness, I was able to come out of that depression. I fought with myself until I did not feel anything anymore. I felt better and learned important lessons in life through experience. I firmly believe things happen for a reason. I encourage young girls to pay close attention to guys' behavior and always follow their instinct.

I thought about so many things in that time of depression. I knew I was not in a healthy relationship due to all the facts. He was over-possessive, always tried to control me, cheated on me, and always lied to me. I knew I left him for all the right reasons, so I do not regret it a bit. I did miss him a lot at times, but time is the greatest of healers, and I decided to trust my timings. I just want you to remember that it is not always all about love. You need to love yourself first before you love someone else. Self-awareness and knowing the exact situation are crucial. Whenever I felt weak, I used to ask myself *why should I run after this guy who cheated on me. I asked myself about the proofs of love he ever gave me*. There were none.

Always remember that the world does not end on one person. Regardless of whoever comes and goes, life goes on. It does not stop for anyone. If you think your partner is toxic, just leave before it is too late. Learn to love yourself and care about yourself. Be confident, and never be afraid to lose anyone who does not appreciate you or thinks you are enough. Cry if you have to and remember that nothing lasts forever. Whatever bad you are going through will be over soon. Wipe your tears, hold your crown, and keep walking this journey of life. Get dressed up, look beautiful. Keep your head up and show the world that you are strong; show them that you are worth everything they are willing to give and beyond.

The struggle, it won't last; but it is up to you, not anyone else.

Chapter 7
Drinking Problems and Crazy Men

A lousy phase does not mean always mean a miserable life. We have to hold on to bad times to realize the value of good times. Though I had had enough hard times that taught me the importance of good times, this phase also taught me that you must not give up because of one wrong chapter in your life. Come what may, we must keep going. There is no choice but to keep moving because life does not stop for anyone or anything.

It is better we accept this fact and keeping pacing forward ourselves than not accepting it and allowing life to force it, thusly making it more miserable. Wherever you are today, and regardless of how badly stuck you feel you are, your story does not end here. Life is full of surprises. You never know what comes next. You cannot just expect every day to be good, so just live every day as it comes.

That is what I decided to do.

After the end of my relationship with that guy, I decided to work on myself. Thinking about myself and my life, I made a decision. I decided to put an end to my drinking habit and live it up. I decided to forget about my past and continue with my life. That is when my life took a U-turn.

My father became more flexible with us and allowed me and my sister to go out and party. After all that had happened, he realized that we were young, and we had the right to have fun as well. We started going to parties at night without worrying about anything. One night my youngest sister and I went to a party where she met a guy. We had a lot of fun together. Everything was so great that night, my sister and this guy that she just met exchanged numbers and became friends.

They started talking on the phone and became really good friends. After being friends for a while, my sister invited him to our house with the approval of my father. We were not allowed to bring anyone home without my father's permission. I recall the day that guy arrived at our apartment, and my sister introduced him to all of us. We had a great night drinking and talking, even dancing. It was a night filled with laughter, and we all had a ball.

Soon after that day, this very guy called my sister and told her that he was impressed by the way I looked. He said he was so interested in getting to know me. When my sister told me, I started to laugh like crazy and said to her that you know well I would not date anyone right now. After what had happened in my previous relationship, there was no way. *"It is not too long ago right now, and the last thing I want is a boyfriend,"* I said.

However, I told her I could speak to him and let him know that I was not into making a relationship then. That is when I found out this guy was married and had a newborn baby. I agreed to speak to him, but things started to get out of hand. He used to send me flower arrangements, and out of nowhere, he appeared everywhere I went. He was just crazy in love or obsessed with me, and believe me, his obsession was getting scary.

This guy was doing everything in his power to get my attention and to get me to say yes to him. He used to stand in front of my house almost every morning but more on Saturdays. He would play music and sing songs declaring his love for me. It was becoming a routine, and whenever he used to stand in front of the house, my sisters and I used to look out through the window and say, *"the crazy guy is here."*

One afternoon, the crazy guy invited me to eat lunch with him. I was tired of running him over, so I agreed to have lunch with him. Oh, boy! I never imagined what happened next. This guy had a plan in his head, and believe me, not a good one. Only if I had known him better, I would never have accepted his invitation in the first place. It was just another horrible day to add to my life's record.

It so happened that he came to pick me up, and I left the house excitedly. My sister told me to send her the details of the place they are going to, just in case. I got into the car, and I asked him, *"So which restaurant are we going?"* He replied, *"It will be a very nice and as beautiful a place as you are,"* to which I smiled and said, *"Seriously!? I need to know the name. My sister told me to tell her the name of the restaurant we go to."* However, he did not disclose the details, not even upon my insistence.

It was a frigid afternoon during the winter of 1994. I used to live close to a cemetery, so he started to drive in that direction. Since I knew that there are no restaurants in that direction, I began to worry. The worry got over me and compelled me to inquire once again. I asked him politely again, *"Which restaurant are we going to? There are no restaurants around this area."* I started to worry and started thinking in my head what is going on with this guy? What is he up to? My heart was beating fast.

After a while, he parked his car on the side of the road and said, first, he would like to talk to me. I told him, *"Okay, so tell me what it is."* Before I could say anything else, all of a sudden, he started to kiss me. I pushed him away and said, *"I am not into any relationship,"* but he did not listen to me and resumed the kiss, holding me tight. Obviously, I did not comply with him. He got outraged and kept kissing me forcefully. I somehow managed to push him away again, and we got into a fight. I managed to get out of his car and started to run as fast as I could. I remember this freaking date like it was just yesterday.

To my disbelief, he started to follow in his car while I was running. He was able to catch me. He grabbed me from my wrist and pushed me into his car. I fought back with this stupid guy as he was trying to kiss me again. I felt like my heart was going to explode. At this point, I did not know what to do. I was out of breathing while my heart was throbbing inside my chest. I was cursing myself for not knowing how gross and desperate this guy was.

Nonetheless, I did not give in to the situation. I was telling myself in my head that I will not give up and let this crazy guy do whatever he is planning to do with me. I was continuously saying, *"Oh, God, help me!!"*

I somehow managed to get off his car again, and I was still running on the road alone. He ran after me, grabbed me from my back very tightly. He was kissing my neck now and telling me, *"You are going to be mine."* I was feeling so disgusted. I once again managed to get out of his grip, and I started to run towards the highway. I ran towards the other side of the road.

At this point, I just wanted to throw myself on the highway. The crazy guy was on the other side, telling me not to do it. He promised me that he would not do it again. I was debating with him if I should jump and die. I was debating if I should believe him or not.

After a good 20 minutes of screaming my head off, I finally decided to cross back over and told him to help me to get back home. I was screaming for so long, but no one cared. No one heard me, and there was no one to help me. By now, my clothes, face, hands, everything else was all so dirty. He said he would not do anything to me. It was evident that he lied to me. Soon after I extended my hand to him, and we started to walk, the nasty bastard grabbed me again from my waist so tight and started to kiss me again. At this point, I kicked his private part and started to run again. I started running hastily and fell, but quickly got up since he was after me.

Oh my God, I was yelling for help, but no one could hear me. I was so desperate for sitting somewhere to catch my breath. The only good thing was that I was not so far from my home. He jumped in his car and started following me again. He kept shouting that one day I will be his woman. I continued running while he kept saying all these crazy things to me, *"Oh my God! God, help me, please!!"* I was screaming until I was able to get back home.

When I got inside the home, my older sister was waiting for me, and she was so worried when she saw me the way I looked. My hair and clothes were all messed up. She was so in shock and asked me, *"What happened to you? Why do you look this way?"* I was so terrified at that time. I did not know what to tell her, so I just started to cry. I cried so much that I could not breathe. My sister waited until I calmed down. Soon after, I told her what happened. She could not believe that I went through all this. She could not believe how that guy could be this horrible and dared to harass me.

The one thing my older sister said to me was the advice that we do not tell anything to my father because we knew he will get furious and will probably kill this guy. Therefore, we decided to keep this as our top secret. The worst part is that the bastard came back to my house, and I had to pretend that nothing happened because I did not want my father to know anything.

He had manipulated my father to like him a lot because he was very well-spoken. He liked to read books and always had a topic to talk to my father. My father never knew about anything that had happened between us. I was so depressed about the situation, and since I could not say anything to my father, he continued with the harassment. I was so pissed for not being able to do anything about it. I went to church, asking God to help me with the situation I was in. I was so desperate to get rid of that crazy guy that I did not know what to do. I was willing to do everything I could to kick him out of my life. I just turned to God to show me the right path.

It was nearly the end of winters, and he continued to harass me. I could not go to the police because I did not want my father to know about it. Just when I felt I was helpless, God's help came for me. I believe God always has a better plan for all of us. If you are in a situation where you think you cannot ever be healed or helped, remember that it is God turning things darker to throw a surprise party for you. He is going to show you a miracle one way or the other. When He wills, you get help from the people and places you did not even imagine. From this time onwards, I started to believe that there is always a light at the end of the tunnel.

The year 1994 had ended, and new things were coming on the way for me. I was sure of that. I had the feeling that 1995 was going to be an excellent year for me because I put my trust in God.

In the winter of 1995, I started working in a company. My older sister and I had applied to work in the same company. Since she was older than me and more experienced, I thought she was going to get that job; however, they only hired me. God's plans are always better than ours. We just need to follow our instincts and never force anything. Sooner or later in life, things do fall into place; you only have to wait for the right moment. It was the month of February. Things were starting to look better. I was getting used to professional life. This company that I was working for had a routine of always throwing parties for 'Valentines.' Therefore, I was invited to the party as well. I told my father about it, and he said that he did not want me to attend this party. I begged him to please allow me to go with my sister. I was so tired of my life and badly needed a break. So, I convinced him, and he finally agreed to let us go but on one condition: we needed to be home by 8 pm, not a second later than that. My father was too much, I know.

The day came, and it was a Friday. It was Friday, the 10th of February, 1995. I recall my youngest sister came to pick me up from the office, and we headed towards the restaurant where Valentine's party was supposed to be. It was not very far from our apartment, so we walked ourselves there. While crossing this one street on our way, right at the corner, we saw there was a young girl. She worked with me and was standing with the guy who I had not seen before. They were talking while pointing towards my sister and myself, which I felt was weird. I asked my sister, *"Did you see them pointing at us?"* she replied, *"Yes, well, let's just walk. Who cares?"*

We got to the restaurant, and soon after, a nice-looking guy walked in. It was the same guy I saw at the corner of the street talking to the girl. He caught my attention at the very moment he walked in. I kept looking at him, which I could not figure out why. That had never happened to me before. There was something about him, or maybe I was attracted to him instantly.

To my surprise, he approached me and introduced himself to my sister and me. The early night went on, and he asked me to dance with him. I said okay and joined him on the dance floor. It was so funny because I considered myself a great dancer, and he did not know how to dance that well, so I told him, *"Let's just sit down. I don't feel like dancing."* We kept talking for a while. Soon, the clock struck eight, and we felt like Cinderella. It was time for my sister and me to go home to not upset my father.

We left, and after walking one block from the restaurant, I heard a voice call my name. We looked back, and it was that guy calling my name. He approached us and said, *"Why you guys left and did not say good-bye to me?"* I said, *"Well,*

I do not know who you are, why should I have said bye?" He asked me for my house number at the time, which I refused to share. *"No, I would not give you my number. Just give me yours,"* I said, and he did.

After thinking a lot, I called him back three days later. He picked up on the second ring, and I could feel the happiness in his voice to hear from me. It was something so weird that we just met at a party, talked for a while, and this guy was so in love with me right at first sight. He was so respectful, kind, caring, and loving with me that I could not help but like him more. I was enjoying the attention this guy was giving me. He wanted to bring all the stars in the sky down for me if it was possible.

We started dating one and a half months later after we met back in 1995. Everyone knew about our relationship, so it was normal for him to come to my place to chill. One day, we were sitting in my living room when the crazy guy called me again to harass me. Guess what? I handed the phone to my boyfriend, who was sitting next to me. He put his mind in place, and this guy never bothered me again.

Like I said before, God always has a better plan for each one of us. When I decided to let go of my previous boyfriend, I did not realize at that time that I made the best choice of my life. I did not follow my heart; I followed my instinct, not knowing it was the best for me. Things happen for a reason. Look at how I met this guy who did not even work in this company, but his friend asked him to come to the party to see me. Who knew we were going to start dating? I decided to give myself another chance, trying not to let bad experiences in my life to affect my belief in the world's good.

Things happen for a reason, and I learned that after all the struggle. Most importantly, I believed in myself, which is what kept me going. I did not close my eyes and my brain to the bad things in life. I learned to let go. As much as I hated my ex-boyfriend and that crazy guy for what they did to me, you can imagine how difficult it would have been for me to let go of all that hate, but I did. I forgive those who do wrong to me. I only wish them the best in this life. I was at peace with myself. I freed myself to enjoy and love my life. I did not allow one bad experience to walk with me for the rest of my life. However, that made me very strong and sturdy. It taught me how to stand tall and how never to let anything make you weak, and I promised myself not to allow any man to walk over me ever again.

The key takeaway here is that everything happens for a reason and at the right moment. You only have to be patient enough to wait for your time to come.

Chapter 8
Marriage

Marriage, to me, was an alienated concept. I was not ready for it when it came to me, but eventually, things worked out. This guy who I was dating for a while now changed my life completely. He was so loyal and fun to be around that I could not help but fall for him even more with each passing day. He always tried his best to make me feel special and never stayed back from making sure I was safe. He always apologized when things went wrong. He was perfect in all senses.

At the back of my heart, I hoped he wants to be with me forever. I was so impressed by his personality because I was not expecting anything like that to happen to me after all the horrible experiences I had had with men before. This was beyond my expectations.

To be honest, my trust in men was at zero when I met this guy, but there was something about him that made me feel that there are some good men left in this world. Everything about him, particularly his maturity and learning about his culture, got all of me. All this curiosity that I have within me did nothing but made me feel that he was the only guy I could imagine the rest of my life with. Oh my God, I was so attracted to him; I had not felt that way in ages.

Since everyone knew about our relationship and my family liked him, my fiancé would often come to my house to meet me. He treated my siblings, my father, and everyone else with great respect, and that is what I liked most about him. One day I when out we him, when I can home my father was drunk. My father was so protected and took him my poor boyfriend again the wall. Oh my God, hold him by his neck and told him if you ever do anything to my daughter that she will cry, you will really know who I am. He was respectful that he did not really know what to do but to said he love me and he will never hurt me. Afterwards my father just didn't want no want to hurt my feelings again. One day we were sitting at my house living room area, we had a conversation where he wanted me to move in with him. I liked the idea, but, in my family, things were quite different. My father would have never allowed me, so I straightaway denied.

I saw his facial expressions changing as if he was more

hurt than disappointed. After thinking for a while, I don't know what came into his mind; he again said to me, *"You know what? I have thought about it so much, and I like you a lot. I cannot imagine my life without you, so I want to marry you. I never want to lose you. You are that perfect woman that I have always wanted. It's like you fell from the sky just for me. I don't want to lose you because I don't find people like you every other day, and I if I have to marry you to be with you forever, I will."* I was so overwhelmed by his words; I started to cry. I never imagined that one day I would mean this much to anyone. We were already dating for three months now. We knew we had our differences; he belonged to a different religion and a completely different cultural background. However, there was no stepping back now. Deep down, nonetheless, I was worried things might not work out.

"Remember that I have told you we have different religions, and that is going to become a conflict," I responded.

"I don't really care about that, you told me that you wanted to leave your house married, so I am going to make your dream come true. If you say yes to me now, we are

going to get married, and I will see you with your father walking you down the aisle," He replied.

I was so amazed. I could not believe any of what was happening. I was only nineteen years old, and this guy wanted to marry me. Everything he said that day made me feel as though I was the luckiest woman alive. *'I am going to marry this guy. Even though we had only met three months back, I want to marry him because he makes me feel secure and loved. He is going to be amazing as a husband, just like my father. I am not going to struggle, and I am going to have a good life,*' I thought.

This guy and the kind of love he had for me was what I was exactly looking for. I craved to have security. I wanted to be with a man that I was sure would keep me safe, the man who will not break my heart and make me struggle because I had already had enough of it. I wanted to trust my instincts this time. I was sure that I am finally going to have somebody who is going to protect me. After moments of thinking and imagining these scenarios, I said, *"Yes, we are going to get marrie*d." I was so excited and euphoric that day.

Nevertheless, things do not always go as planned in this ever-changing world. There came our first hurdle hitting us hard. My fiancé was afraid to tell his mother about us because our religions were different, and they were very much of their own kind. I said to him, *"We can go together and tell your mother."* Giving you all a little background, I was born in a Catholic religion, back in Dominican Republic. My native language is Spanish, whereas he was an Indian Muslim who was born in Guyana, South America.

After giving it a thought, we went to his house, and that is when I realized he lived quite far away from me. He lived near Long Island, and still come to my house to see me almost every single day, which involved an hour of traveling to and from my home each way. He traveled by train, which even stretched the ride to about an hour and a half. I was amazed again. He did not miss a single chance to amaze me. He was effortlessly fabulous due to his selflessness. Anyhow, we went to his mother, and I initiated the conversation. I told his mother what we both were up to, and then he joined the chat. His mother said, "*You guys just met! This is too soon."* She did not really care about the differences. He then told his mom, *"This is what I want. I don't want to lose this woman. If I don't marry her now, I think I am going to lose her."*

Soon, his brother was getting married too. So, his mother said, *"Okay, if this is the decision you guys want to make, fine. One more time, are you sure you want to do this?"* That is when I realized that she was not so hard to convince. She was just concerned about both of us since we had just met a couple of months back and were too young. Besides that, my boyfriend already had a daughter, his mother was concern about that as well. It was a critical condition, but I was sure I wanted to do this because I wanted to feel free. Since my father was so strict, he would not let me go out. I could not go to the club. I could not do so many things on my own. I thought I would have a little freedom if I get married. I wanted to get married because there were so many things that I could not do as a single woman. I wanted to do everything with my future husband, which I could not do before. Of course, this was not the only reason I wanted to get married. I just did not want to lose the amazing human that he was.

Now that his mother was convinced, it was time for me to tell my family about it. I had not disclosed anything to my father yet, but now I had to tell him because we had already convinced his mother. I still remember the day I told my father about getting married. I was mopping the floor, and he was home doing his work. I just went to him and sat down next to him and said, *"He proposed me for marriage."* My father was in shock. He looked at me and said, *"What are you talking about? Are you crazy?"*

"I am sorry, but I probably am crazy because I want to marry him," I said. *"Are you out of your mind? You are so young - only nineteen years old. You are still in school. What are you talking about?"* He remarked.

"Calm down. You don't have to worry. We are adults, and we know what we are doing. We can get married, and if things do not work out, I can get divorced." I replied. This is the one thing I said that made my father more upset.

"You are not even married yet, and you are thinking about divorce? Are you crazy? You don't say that when you know marriage is forever." He almost shouted.

My father is very traditional, and to him, marriage meant a forever commitment. He was thinking fast and said, *"What kind of marriage are you going to do?"* He was in such a rush that he continued sending questions and assumptions my way. *"Where am I going to get money from? I am pretty sure you want a big wedding,"* He said all at once.

"You don't have to worry. I work, and my boyfriend works, too. Everybody can help us a little. I am not asking you to pay for my wedding." I said, *reassuringly.*

"Okay, so when are you guys getting married?" My father asked.

"Saturday!" I responded excitedly.

"What? Is this a joke? What kind of wedding are you planning for yourself? What do you mean on Saturday?" He said with an evident frown spread across his forehead. I was expecting this reaction, though, and handled it well. Hence I told my father about the marriage on Wednesday June 20, 1995.

Things were going rather fast, but I did not doubt anything for a second. The funny thing is that a lot of people from the place I worked at knew him. He used to come to this place and meet every single young girl that used to work there. Everyone used to say to me, *"You are just another person in his life. He is probably going to play around, and he is not going to marry you."*

I remember one of these ladies from work who told me that if he marries me, she will buy me the wedding invitations and all the wedding accessories that were needed at that time. She even said, *"I am going to buy all these things for you because I do not believe he is going to marry you."* When we finally made that decision, she bought everything for the wedding, as per her promise, including all the accessories, wedding invitation, and napkins. Smoking in the parties was common back then, so she bought us ashtrays as well as their matches. Everything had our names etched on it and the color I picked myself.

In the same week, when I told my father, my boyfriend came to my house and proposed to me officially. It was Friday evening. Everyone was eventually happy about it. We had champagne. I invited my aunts and everybody else. My father was also happy afterward. He said, *"What can I say? If that is something you want to do, I don't want to stop you even though you are taking a risk because you have only known this guy for three months."* I replied, saying, *"I know I am taking the risk, but I feel that everything is going to be fine. My instinct is telling me that everything is going to be okay."*

My fiancé then asked my father, *"I want to marry your daughter. Would you allow me to do so?"* My father said, "Yes." Everything after that was like a fairytale. The next day, Saturday, I got married to the love of my life. It was in June 1995. I got married according to the Muslim faith, which in itself was amazing. However, I did not stay with him. I came back to my house the next day. His family was like, *"Where are you going?"* and I said, *"I am going back home."* The reason I came back is that we did the wedding according to Muslim rituals to please his family, especially to make his mother happy. However, I wanted to have the wedding according to my religion, too. We had mutually decided that we will have a big wedding in September. From the day we got married, we only had four months to prepare for the big wedding. My older sister played her role of being the elder very well. She was a huge part of it all helped me a lot to prepare for the wedding. We don't know how, but the four months went by too fast. Finally, the day came, and we got married on September 16, 1995.

It was such a beautiful day. I had bridesmaids. Everyone was involved, and everyone loved everything so much. We got all the attention and affection. My husband and I decided that we wanted to have a wedding in which we can invite everyone without any restrictions. We wanted to have a traditional wedding.

We had at least 200 people at the wedding, and everyone was treated well. Since it was a union of two different cultures and religions, we had two types of cuisines at the wedding. We had Indian food as well as Spanish. His part of the family was there, and so was mine. Everything seemed great. We also had a singer at our wedding. Everyone was dancing on both types of music. It was such a beautiful thing to witness. I remember when the priest announced us as husband and wife, I could not stop laughing. I was laughing non-stop, and everyone else started to laugh too. I don't really know why I was laughing. Maybe I remembered the lady who said he wouldn't marry me, or it was the fact that I was only nineteen and already married. The only thing that mattered at the time was that I was so happy. At this point, my husband and I were together for seven months. Of course, we signed the papers as well, so we were married legally now. That's when our happy story continues. We were finally going to move in together and start a life.

We had planned so many things that we would do together, just like every other couple does. We decided not to have any children until we get to know each other fully. We wanted to enjoy ourselves before we start a family. We also planned that we were only going to have a baby only when both of us agreed that it was the right time to have one. We had a lot to do before that. I had to finish school and go to college. He was my biggest motivation. That was the thing about him that I liked. He always wanted to help me go in the right track. He was like a mentor to me. He balanced my life. When he knew that I was off the track, he would always bring me back on it. He would say things like, *"What are you doing? Are you crazy?"* He remained in charge because he was the mature one among us, and I was always doing crazy stuff.

Deep down, I knew he was going to support me in all my crazy ideas. I just knew that this man was going to turn me into a better person, better than who I was. I am a little bit hyper, a little wild, and I like to do all the crazy stuff in the world. That is one thing that he said he loved about me - my craziness and how I am always like a free bird. Contrarily, he was and still is like a mixture of both. He lets me be free but also knows very well when to pull me back.

Anyway, that is how our life started. I went to college; we traveled together; we dined out and lived our lives to the fullest. We moved into his mother's house after we got married. We had our separate bedroom, and his brother lived in the same house. His mother was very nice. Since we got married so soon, we did not have the time to look for an apartment. The idea was to move into his mother's house and get settled down. However, we lived with his mother for just two years. Soon, we realized that we needed to look for another place to live. Although my husband was very much against it, my physical health started to get affected. His mother also did not want us to move, but then she said she wanted us to stay there for six months, at least. She wanted us to be ready to buy a new house before we moved out. She was very supportive.

The reason we thought of moving out was that things were getting bitter between my brother-in-law's wife and me. That is when I told my husband that I wanted to have my own house. I soon realized that no matter how nice people are, you have to have your own home when you get married. My brother in law used to live in the basement with his wife.

There was a conflict between his wife and myself because I used to work and go to school. Whenever I came back home, I wanted to prepare my meal, but she was always in the kitchen and never left. The kitchen was always dirty because she used to make food there and did not clean timely. One day, she and I got into a heated argument.

Ever since then, I started feeling uncomfortable, and that was when I told my husband to start looking for an apartment. One day, the argument between my sister-in-law and myself got so heated that I got hospitalized because of the heart condition that I had. I passed out that night because the argument was fierce. That was when I told my husband that if we did not decide about moving out, we were getting separate because I could not live there anymore. He was kind of resistant to it, so I clearly said, *"If we do not soon find another place to live, we are going to get separate because I want my separate place and my privacy. I know you want to hang with your parents, and I know you want to be very supportive of them. I also know your mother does not want us to leave because, in her mind, she thinks you are safer here. However, that's not what I am thinking. I think I want to be free to do a lot of things, but most of all, I want my peace of mind."*

I was getting depressed because of the situation. I was going to school and was also working in a company in Manhattan. By the time I used to come home, it was probably around six or seven in the evening. I already used to be exhausted from working hard and school, so I just wanted to lie down in peace. However, none of the things that were happening around me made me feel at peace. The conflicts with this young girl were destroying my peace. The cherry on top, I was the only Spanish in the house. The rest of them were all Indians. I was cooking my separate food. I could not cook food for my husband the way I wanted because of the cultural differences that we had. They do not eat pork. I liked to eat pork but not all the time, of course. I had to respect their culture. I could not walk around the house the way I wanted to. I just got married, come on. Certain things were not possible because I lived in somebody else's house. I felt I have no privacy in their house, and on top of that, that young woman was giving me a rough time.

I encourage people not to spend all their money on having a big wedding and look for an apartment to live in instead. If you ever see yourself involve in this type of situation, you can always have a big wedding later, including all the things that you want to do. It is better to utilize half the money for better accommodation so that you can enjoy your new life… We never used to be home. We rather used to travel a lot, party a lot and enjoy ourselves. At the same time, we were getting prepared to deal with our families. Soon, we were able to convince them about moving out and bought an apartment of our own.

One more thing that I would like to advise here is that don't rush into having families right away so you can have time to figure things out.

Again, he played his role of being the smarter one in my life. I wanted to have a baby from the very beginning. I used to say, *"I want to become a mother,"* and he used to say, *"Hold on. There is no rush. We are still too young."* He was the one who said that we must wait till things are fine, and I was done with my academics. At that time, I was 23.

One thing that I really liked about my husband was that he never made any promises to me before the wedding that I will do this or that. He never makes any promises now even after all these years. Even if I say, *"Promise me,"* he would say, *"No. Let us see what is going to happen tomorrow."*

From the beginning of our relationship, he used to say he was not going to promise me anything because he can never be sure if he would be able to do something. This is how I always know that it is either black or white. There is no grey. He lets me be wild, and on the other hand, he is very calm.

In every marriage, there are ups and downs. Nothing's perfect. There are arguments, there are moments when you don't want to speak to each other, and when you just want to walk away. However, we never left each other ever during our fights. During our first five years of marriage, it did not matter if we argued or not, we were always together. We always talked about everything that bothered us. Just as they say, communication is the key, but comprehending each other was more important. It sure is. No matter what happens, we always communicated what we did not like about each other and still do. That is one thing that is important to me. We would always tell each other what made us upset.

He was sometimes quiet about some things to me because he thought if he told me, I would get more upset than I already was. Nonetheless, I managed to get the word out of his mouth always because I knew imploding is worse than exploding - it is detrimental to relationships. I did, and I still force him to tell me how he feels and what he wants to say.

This way, we know well where we stand in each other's life. Of course, he always says that I am the one to start a fight. There is one thing that I cannot keep myself from saying. It is that the more I learned about Tony and his culture, the more I loved my decision to spend my life with him. I learned about their music and all about their culture, but I did not learn about his religion or the way they cook. They cook a lot of curries. I don't really like curry because it has a lot of spices. Despite these differences, we always stood by each other.

One day, my husband asked me if he wants me to go to his mother's house and learn how to cook their type of food. *"Well, you should have married an Indian woman and not me,"* I said. He loves his food; he loves his culture. That is why I said he should not have married a Spanish woman. "Now that you have married me, we are going to eat the food that I cook because I am the female here. If you want to have your Indian food, you can go to your mother's house, or there are plenty of Indian restaurants available you can buy from, or best, you learn to cook yourself," I said to him. I used to joke around obviously, but he was tolerant enough to the crazy and stupid things I said. That is how things were for the first five years of our marriage. We were leading quite a happy married life. I loved the little world of our own. Then things changed as we decided to start our own family.

"There is no such thing as a broken family." Family is family and is not determined by marriage certificates, divorce papers, and adoption documents. Families are made in the heart. The only time a family becomes null is when those ties in the heart are cut. If you cut those ties, those people are not your family. If you make those ties, those people are your family. And if you hate those ties, those people will still be your family because whatever you hate will always be with you."

-C. JoyBell C.

Chapter 9
Building a Family

'Family' is a single word with many different meanings. How amazing is that we live with multiple people under a single roof, despite the differences, connected to them by an invisible string? All of them have different personalities, and yet all of you get along so well. That is what blood does; it binds people together regardless of their differences. It is a beautiful feeling indeed to have someone with you that you are sure will always be there for you. You know when things go wrong, they will have your back. Having a family is nice, but building a family? It is terrifying.

This chapter is close to my heart because it is about the time when my husband and I decided to grow our family. It was the time we decided to have a child of our own - the time when I decided that I wanted to become a mother. It was a huge responsibility, but I finally felt like I was ready for it.

It all began one beautiful day when my husband and I were sitting in the living room, watching television. It was a typical day in our routine. All of a sudden, my husband gave me a certain look, and he said, *"Don't you think it's time?"* My confused soul asked, *"time for what?" "Time to have a family, to have a baby of our own,"* He replied, and I jumped off the couch with excitement. *"Have WHAT?!"* I said, making my euphoria obvious. He said, *"It's time to have somebody running around the house, a little soul that contains a piece of our hearts, the center of our universe, doing all the crazy stuff as you do. It is time we have a smaller version of you. It feels like we have accomplished so many things together, and we are ready for it. It is high time we start thinking about creating a family."*

I was so happy to hear him say this because I always wanted to have a baby. Therefore, no more protection, although I just finished college, I wanted to go back. *"Yes! It is a great idea. It is amazing to become parents,"* I said. Though my husband already had a daughter from his previous relationship, we were equally excited. Obviously, we needed to have a baby of our own. I still remember how I planned every little thing perfectly. I wanted the baby to be born in the summers, basically in June, so we planned everything accordingly. I went to my doctor, and he said everything was fine with me. I could conceive, so we went ahead to start the family. Everything was going smoothly. I woke up each day excited, thinking maybe it is the day I get the good news? I checked myself every month excitedly, and each time I would go like, *"Oh my God! I am pregnant!!"* only to realize not yet.

Usually, when you become pregnant, you find out at least four weeks later because you usually check yourself when you miss your period. Therefore, one morning, I woke up and realized I had missed my periods. I did a pregnancy test immediately, and I found out that finally, I was pregnant. I was so damn excited because I did not ever take any birth control pills or hormonal pills to prevent myself from pregnancy. However, I used to use natural methods to prevent becoming pregnant, and it gave me some kind of peace. I was 23 years old, a perfect age to be able to carry a baby and give birth.

I was so happy to know that I was going to have a baby that I called everyone over for a party. I have a habit of celebrating little things that bring everyone together, especially when something like this happens. I think I got this from my mom; she always used to see her sibling for no reason and loved watching everyone together and happy. I also wanted to have a get-together where I break the news and go like, *"I have a surprise for you all."* Everyone was present at my father's house when I made the announcement that I was going to have a baby. Everyone was equally excited because we had been married for five years now, and whenever I met anyone anywhere, they would go like, *"When are you guys going to have a baby?"* At least I would not have to answer those questions anymore.

My sister, who was sick, forgot about her disease and became happy in my happiness. She could not believe I was going to be a mother like her. Everything was so thrilling. One evening, my sister called me and told me that she was in a very critical condition and needed help. I got so worried that I hung up the phone and ran towards her house, which was almost 20 blocks away from my apartment. I could not take a car, so I decided to run myself there because she was sick and I was really worried.

As I was running, I felt like something dropped inside of me, and in my head, I was like, "Oh My God! Is my baby okay?" but I did not pay much attention to it because at that time I was only concerned about my sister. I was ten weeks pregnant then. Everything was fine with my sister, thankfully. I did not feel anything weird afterward, but then the next day, I started to have severe pain in my stomach's left side. I knew something was not right.

I immediately went to the hospital. I was in so much pain and was praying to God to keep my baby safe, but soon, I found out that I lost my baby. It was devastating.

They did a sonogram, and then they told me they could not hear any heartbeat. I shouted, *"How is that possible? I did not even bleed?"* I was under the impression that when you lose a baby, you start bleeding. I said, *"I just had pain on my stomach's left side, and that is it."* The doctor said, *"We are sorry, ma'am! The baby's heart stopped responding. Even if you had this baby, it was not going to be normal. There are some problems with your hormones."* I felt like the ground was slipping below my feet. I was thinking to myself, *"No!! What am I going to tell everyone? What am I going to do now? What is going to happen?"*

They sent me home afterward. I remember it was one cold Friday of December 1999. They said to me, *"Go home, rest for a while, then come back to us on Monday."* I went back home, and as soon as I saw my elder sister, I hugged her and cried like never before. My elder sister tried her best to calm me down, then she said to me, *"Why don't you go to another hospital and get a second opinion?"* However, I was in a huge shock that I lost my first child. My brain was not comprehending the situation, and I was not in the position to go to another hospital and get myself checked.

I was crying profusely. I locked myself in a room and did not talk to anyone. On Monday, I went to see my doctor. I was still hoping that this news turns out to be false. I was hoping doctors would say it was a misunderstanding, but it was not. It was a living nightmare. When I reached the hospital, I found out that the doctor had called me again only to remove the baby, which was still there inside my body. The doctors had to do a D and C, which is the process of removing the baby after a miscarriage. I could not help but cry my heart out. It was too painful for me to bear. My heart was shattered in pieces. Those pieces were stinking inside my womb in the form of my first baby that I had just lost. It was the weakest I had ever been. It made me feel as though anything that I loved too much went far away from me. I went into a deep depression again.

The doctors told me that I had to wait at least 5 to 6 months to be able to conceive again. It was the time that my body needed to heal from the trauma it had just been through. I was so scared that what if I get pregnant again before the right time? I was afraid of losing my child again. I used to cry to my husband every single day. One day, he sat down with me and said, *"I want you to stop crying, remembering what happened. We can have another baby. The worries are never going to end. I just want you to be positive and get over it."* I was so scared, *I asked him, "What if we lose the other baby too?"* Everything that had happened left a huge impact on me.

As I said at the beginning of this book, life is never a bed of roses for anyone. There are always ups and downs. Though my husband was very nice, pregnancy is not the only thing I struggled with. Since I was the only Spanish in the house, my accent was quite different from my husband's rest of the family. I remember we used to gather at my husband's family house at the weekends, and his family used to make fun of my accent. They used to play around with words and indirectly bully me. They used to think I was stupid enough not to figure it out, and it used to hurt me so much. I am bringing this up here because this problem needs to be addressed. Just because I did not want myself to go into any kind of inferiority complex, I used to tell myself that I have this accent because I am Spanish, and I did not grow up in this country. I came here after puberty, and when you pass puberty and learn any other languages, you cannot have the speaker's accent. Still, I never gave up, and I used to tell myself that I will work on my accent and make it better. Up until this age, there are certain words that I cannot pronounce clearly. I roll my tongue, I guess. However, I made a promise to myself that I am going to learn English and would improve my accent. It's unbelievable how adults, in this case, can be so immature; however, as much as it used to bother me, I never gave up or got intimidated. I continued to learn English despite my accent, and I am very proud of it.

Time flew by, and after the dark, long stormy night came the beautiful morning. I became pregnant again. I was so happy and could not contain my happiness. I went back to the same hospital where I lost my 1st pregnancy. For some reason, I felt inside my heart that the baby that I had lost was still alive. I don't know why I just had this suspicion. They did a sonogram and then said to me, *"There is something wrong with your hormones. It looks like you are going to lose the baby again."* This made me depressed again, but inside my heart, I told myself that *no, this time, it is not going to let this happen again. I am not going to allow them to take my baby out*, I thought. As said before, I also had this feeling that the baby they took out was still alive. I just knew right then that there is something wrong. This was the moment I decided to better go to another hospital for a second opinion. I wanted to make no mistake this time because I wanted my first child to enter this world.

The next day I went to the same hospital, it was the same doctor. She said to me, *"Come see me tomorrow. We are going to do hormone testing. You have a meager count, and I am afraid this is going to affect the baby and the process of its development. We have to run a few tests urgently."* I told her, *"Okay! No problem, I will be back,"* and never went back. I went to another hospital instead and explained everything that had happened with me to that other doctor. That is when she cleared my mind and said, *"No. Sometimes you can lose a baby, which is terrible. Sometimes, there are some problems with the hormones due to which the baby does not develop, and its heartbeat stops."* It quite cleared my mind, but for some reason, my heart still felt my first child was alive, and I felt it was a girl. The feeling was horrifying. Days were passing by with me going in and out of the hospitals. When they did the sonogram in my second pregnancy, the doctors said they could not see the baby, but they could see the sack. They said that they could see I was pregnant, but they could not see the baby clearly. My heart dropped. I said, *"Please don't tell me I lost this baby too."* The doctor told me, *"Let's wait another month. Don't jump to conclusions. Sometimes the baby is so tiny that they can hide, and you are unable to see them in the sonogram."* Her words somehow gave me hope, and I decided to wait for another month. I prayed to God for things to turn out well in the end.

A month passed. I went back to the hospital again for my appointment. My heart was beating so fast when they did a sonogram again. Fortunately, they could see the baby this time and feel its heartbeat. I was so much relieved and happy. However, they said this pregnancy is going to be full of risks. My stress level at the moment was so high because my sister was sick, I was going to school, and I was working as well. So many things were going on in my life at a time. My pregnancy was high-risk because I had heart surgery when I was a child. My heart used to beat very fast for some reason.

I guess because two hearts were pumping. Also, I was anemic; my red blood cells were deficient.

The doctor said, *"You need to be relaxed and calm. The stress is not good for you and the baby."* That's when I made a decision. I decided to quit my job. I talked to my husband, and he supported my decision. It was the best thing I could do at the moment. I wanted to take all the possible precautions because I did not want to lose my child this time. Therefore, I stopped working, and everything was going well. I remember when it was time for me to find out if it was a boy or a girl. I was extremely excited. I always used to say that whenever I have a baby, I want a boy. So, they did the final sonogram, and the doctor said, *"Are you ready to know what you got in there?"* and I said, *"Yes!"* She said, *"You are having a boy!"* I cannot describe in words how happy I was.

I was so excited that I started looking for a name for my child. One day, I was in my living room watching TV, and I saw a Spanish actor whose name was John Sebastian. I saw another singer; whose name is Justin Timberlake. I liked their names a lot, so I decided to combine them and come up with a name for my child. I decided to name my child Justin

Sebastian, and that is how the name was decided. When I told my husband the name that I chose, he agreed to it. However, when his family got to know the name of my child, they were not too happy about it. I wanted my son to have 'Sebastian' for his first name, but my husband's family used to say Sebastian from the movie "Little Mermaid," in which the lobster's name was "Sebastian." This hurt me a lot, and I was really upset about it. However, I did not let them ruin my happiness, and I said I am still going to name my son whatever I want to because that is my child, and as long as I am comfortable with the name, I don't care what anyone else has to say.

Their words bothered me and affected my mental health a lot. That is why I say that sometimes people do not realize how much they can affect someone with the things they say, especially when we are adults. We do not think even for a second. We do not think what impact our words might have on someone. We do not know what they are going through and how depressed they already are. We don't think it's because the person is very sensitive. No, not at all. We just need to be careful about how we express ourselves. This is something that I have learned throughout my life that we, as humans, have to be very careful while speaking to others. I am the type of person that if I want to say something to someone, I am as honest as possible. At the same time, though, I also make sure that I do not hurt their feelings.

There is always a way of speaking the truth. Even if people are wrong, I know how to let them know without pulling them down. I would never deliberately hurt someone's self-esteem because I have been through it, and I know how it feels. Imagine a lady, who is just about to have her first baby, decides a name for it, and suddenly everyone starts making fun of it. I will never say that what you are doing is wrong directly, I will say maybe what you are doing is right, but there could be many other ways of doing the same thing. This is what I mean when I say that watch out your words when you speak to other people. I honestly judge people by the way they talk to others; it tells a lot about their personality.

Joking around is fine, but if you know that the other person has feelings about something and it is going to hurt them, it is better not to say anything at all. This is even more important when you are frank with that person, but just be careful how frank you are going to be. Also, when a woman is pregnant, she gets very sensitive towards things. Therefore, when they joked about the name of my baby, I just could not take it. All I said was, *"If you do not like the name, it is okay because as long as I like it, I don't care about anyone else."*

I was kind of upset while I was pregnant. Besides, I also almost got hit by a car. I was walking on the road, thinking about everything. I did not realize a car was coming in my direction. People around me shouted, *"Watch out Lady!!"* and I looked around and moved back just in time. The car almost hit me while it scurried. I was going to cross the street, but thankfully, I was safe, and so was the fetus inside.

Months went by, and the day came when I had my baby shower. I still remember we threw a massive party for it. Everyone was pretty excited. However, nobody knew it's a boy. Even though I used to say if I have a boy, I am going to name him Sebastian, I had to choose the name for a girl too.

Only my husband and I knew that we were going to have a baby boy. Therefore, what we did, we chose two colors for the theme of the baby shower; pink and blue. We did not tell anyone what I was having until the baby was born. Everyone was going crazy about it, talking about what it was going to be. It was so overwhelming. But the day finally came. I could not believe I was a mother now. I was attached to him through the invisible strings I talked about from the day he was born.

A lot of our relatives would come to my house to see the baby, and they would touch it with their cold hands. It bothered me so much, which was ridiculous. Keeping in mind that I lost a child before I had my first baby, I was very protective of him. I never left him alone with anyone.

I loved him to the core of my heart. It was like my entire world revolved around him. I took great care of him, and my husband loved him so much that he would always bring things for him on his way back home from work. Then came a day in our lives that when I think about it, it just shatters me down. When my son was a year and a half, I almost lost him. I recall that day when I went to pick him up from daycare. After being home for almost two years, taking care of my son, I had put him in daycare because I had to go for job interviews since I was looking for work.

Therefore, I picked him up and decided to go and pick my husband from his office as well so that we could go back home together. It was almost time for him to leave. While I was close to my husband's office, I was hit by a car while crossing the road. My heart skipped a beat, thinking what if it had hurt my son? Thank God, I was walking without a stroller. Before we crossed the street, my son wanted to walk by himself, and I said, "No, let me carry you." I made that decision because I knew if something happened to him, I would lose my mind. Thank God, I decided to hold him in my arms. The car threw me 20 to 30 feet to the side from the middle of the road. About the baby, the witnesses say that I lifted my child in the air, and I took all the pressure from the car on myself. My neck was fractured. I was supposed to get surgery later, but I never did because it was very complicated. So, sometimes my neck gets swollen.

When I do a lot of lifting work, it starts aching. Thank goodness, though, nothing happened to my child. I could not afford another loss. I fractured my leg and broke my toes. The doctors had to put a cast on my leg. I could not walk for two months, but at least my child was safe. They had to do surgery on one of my knees.

And I had to go through therapy. During the time of going to therapy, I was sexually harassed by one of the dentists. He grabbed one of my breasts while I was sitting on the chair being checked. The doctor asked the assistant to grab something for him and that's when he decided to do that. It was a very uncomfortable moment for me, so you can imagine the commotion that occurred. The doctor said his hand slipped and it was an accident he did not mean to do. "Yeah alright," I just left things as they were. I had too much going on.

So many things can happen in our life. But one thing I did not realize back then that it was another blessing in disguise for me; I was blessed and happy that my son was saved. That car could have hit my son, and if it did, he would not have survived. But thank God he was saved; I did not find even a single scratch on his body. Let me tell you one thing, God is great. He did not let anything happen to my son. My whole body was hit by a car. I was underneath, and I was holding the baby up in the air with my two bare hands without letting go. Everyone was yelling, *"Oh my God!"* I did not know I was the one who was hit by the car until I saw people gathering around me because it all happened in the blink of an eye. It took me time to recover from all the injuries, but I will always be grateful to God for not letting anything happen to my son. Everything was going well, and when my son was four years old, I decided I wanted to have another baby.

However, what I did not know is that I had problems to conceive another baby. I remember going to the hospital and asking the doctor, *"We are trying to have a baby. I am not using anything harmful, and the process is natural. I am still unable to conceive, what is going on with me?"* She checked me and said, *"Nothing is wrong; everything is fine with you. Don't rush. Such delicate things take time."*

Things started to get ugly because I started thinking that if everything is fine with me, there must be something wrong with my husband. I wanted to have another baby so bad due to which we used to argue a lot. I would tell my husband that the doctor said everything is fine with me, so I wanted him to go and get himself checked. I started putting a lot of pressure on my husband to go to the doctor. There came the point where I told my husband that I wanted to divorce him. I was so upset that he was not even trying. I thought he did not want to have any more children. I was severely depressed because I could not become a mother again. I used to tell my husband, *"Maybe it's because of you, and it's your fault. I don't want to be with you because then I cannot have*

173

babies." You see, I was going crazy because my son was so sad since he did not have any siblings to play with. My husband calmed me down and said he would get himself checked.

Finally, we decided to go to the doctor. I was so embarrassed when I had to tell the doctor that I want my husband to be checked because my doctor kept saying that everything is fine with me. He recommended us to the Urologist. They ran all kinds of tests on my husband, and they all turned out fine. Everything was perfect with him. I had never been relieved and stressed at the same time in a single situation before that day.

Then after we came back home, he threw the test results on my face saying, *"Everything is fine with me. I don't have any problem, you are the one with the problem,"* and I said, *"I don't have any problem either because the doctor did not say anything to me about that."* This went on for days we argued every other day.

One day, one of my cousins came over to see me, and I expressed to her what was going with me. She recommended me to go see a doctor, so after hearing everything that I was going through, she said to me, *"Why don't you go and get a second opinion?"* and I said, *"Why should I? The doctor that I am seeing is an expert in this field. She is in the news for being the best doctor, so why go for a second opinion?"*

However, I thought about it, and I decided to see my doctor once again. I went to her and said, *"Listen! I am trying. I am trying so hard, but it is not happening."* Just like always, she would give me advice about what I should and should not do, including all the home remedies and precautions that I was already practicing, but nothing worked. She said, *"Jocelyn! I am checking everything, and everything is fine. What I am going to do is I am going to send you to a special fertilize clinic. Maybe they can check your hormones and everything else with much more focus to see if everything is okay with you."*

My insurance did not cover the procedure I was recommended by my doctor. When I called to find out how much it was, it was a lot of money. I started getting depressed because my only son was home alone with me, and he wanted to have a brother or a sister. I did not know how to explain to him that I could not have any babies and that I was having so much trouble. I did not dare to tell him that I could not get him as a brother or sister. Besides, he had a sister, but she lived somewhere else so he could not spend time with her. He had cousins too, but still, it was not the same. I was always sad and depressed, and watching my son playing all by himself always broke my heart.

I remember my cousin called again to know how things were, and she again said, *"Please go see this doctor for a second opinion." After so many years passed* finally, I listened to my cousin, I went to the doctor for the second opinion, and that is when I found that I had Endometriosis. It is a condition caused when the tissue (endometrium) that normally lines the uterus begins growing outside of the uterus and creates a wall inside the uterus. The condition can cause a lot of symptoms, and one of them is the difficulty of becoming pregnant, pelvic pain, several cramps during or before menstruation, infertility, and so on. I was in constant pain.

I told the doctor all the symptoms that I had, and he said, *"You have Endometriosis, but I want to make sure how severe it is. The doctor said; I'm going to insert a camera inside of your uterus and fallopian tube so we can see what can be done about it."* Fast forward ten years today, my older son is ten years old and has no sibling. So, all these years, I was trying to become a mother again, and nothing worked.

When the doctor said to me that I have that condition, he said it is nothing to be worried about. However, it was tough for me to conceive a child with this condition. He wanted to put me through the hormonal treatment to help me, but I am very much against putting anything unnatural inside my body. I said, *"No! I am not taking any medication or any kind of treatment."* I never want to put anything inside my body that I know must have side effects. I refused to do the hormonal treatment, because it was only going to help me with the pain and nothing else. *"I put it in God's hands, and He is going to decide if I am going to have another child or not."*

Of course, I was very depressed. It had come to the point that I did not want to have any romantic relationship with my husband. This was because I wanted to have a child, and I was depressed as I was unable to have another child. I was like, 'what is the purpose of doing it if I am not going to have any children?' I was being ignorant as well. It was really affecting our relationship.

I went to the doctor again and said to him, *"I want you to recheck my uterus and tubes because I am having a lot of pain, and I don't know what to do."* When he checked again, he said to me, *"Jocelyn! I have terrible news for you. "You are not going to be able to have any more children. Your condition is so severe that at this point, all I can say is you cannot conceive." However, I think you need some cleaning in your tubes. There is so much blockage in there that I need to clean it a little bit. But unfortunately, I don't think you are going to become a mother again."*

Wow!!!! I was depressed again and called my youngest sister. She cried when I told her about my condition, and I started crying too. She told me not to worry, and things will be better. She was given me so much support so I could feel better. I remember my doctor told me, *"Just leave it up to God. He is the only one who makes that decision."* Deep down, however, I knew I was done. Therefore, I decided to swallow the bait; I accepted the fact that I probably will not have any more children, and I stopped thinking about it. As I told earlier, I am the kind of person who always wants to have a meeting and communicate everything to the ones who matter, because communication is very important to me.

When I came home, I sat with my husband and my only son. I was continuously crying. I could barely breathe, but I gulped it all down, and I told them that the doctor said I was not going to be able to become a mother again. My son started crying. He was really upset about it, but my husband said, *"Don't worry. It is what it is. It is okay if we are not going to have any more children. We already have one, and we should be grateful."* He is very practical and also very supportive. I said, *"Yeah, but I wanted my son to have a brother too."* Nonetheless, I left this whole thing alone and stopped thinking about it.

Three Months Later...

Guess What? Okay, let us maintain a little bit more suspense. It was one regular day. My son, my husband, and I were all sitting together, watching TV. I just was not feeling well. Everything that I ate or drank, I felt like it was spoiled. Everything tasted like onions to me. I had terrible mood swings that day, and all of a sudden, my husband said to me, *"Maybe you are pregnant!"* I was like, *"Please! Don't start all this again. You know the doctor said I could not have any more children. How can I be pregnant?"* He was like, *"Remember; he said only God could make this happen?"* So,

179

I gave it a thought and said, *"Okay, get me a couple of pregnancy test strips."*

He bought some and I bought some for myself. I checked myself with my heart beating very fast inside my chest, and guess what? The test turned out positive. I was like, 'Nooo! This can't be true,' because they said I could not have any more children, but I remembered what the doctor had said. He said, *"Only God makes this decision!"* God truly is magical.

By the grace of God, I became pregnant again. I could not believe that I was pregnant. I went to the pharmacy and bought six pregnancy test strips, and to my surprise, they all came out positive. My husband was not home when I ran the tests. It was just my son and me. We started jumping like crazy while hugging each other, crying and screaming at the same time, *"Oh My God!! We are going to be parents again! You are going to have a brother!! You are going to have a sister!!"* We were so excited!! When my husband came home, he asked us, *"Why are you both jumping like monkeys? What happened?"* and I showed him all the pregnancy tests, and said while sobbing, *"I am going to have a baby again!"* His expressions changed to complete joy, but he did not want to be disappointed again. We were tired of touching the moon only to realize it was just an illusion.

All he said to me was, *"I don't believe you!"* and I said, *"Look at all the pregnancy tests, man!"* He said, *"I still don't believe you. What are we going to do?" "What do you mean, what are we going to do? WE ARE GOING TO HAVE A BABY!"* I said. We were all going so crazy; it was finally a happy day after so many sad days.

The next day I went to the hospital, and I pretended that I was having a lot of pain in my stomach. I did not say anything to the doctors. I did not tell them I was pregnant. I said, *"I am having a lot of pain in my abdomen. I need to be checked."* So, they immediately did a sonogram and asked me, *"Are you aware that you are pregnant?"* And I was like, *"YESS!! I KNOW!"* The doctor said, *"Congratulations!"* I did this because I just wanted to make sure it was true and that I was not dreaming about becoming a mother again. I need to thank my cousin, who convinced me to get a second opinion. She became the Godmother of my second child. Time past and I delivered my second healthy baby. Afterward, my condition got worse. It got worse to the point that I had to remove my uterus and tube, after which I could not conceive any more children. But that's okay because I was happy and grateful that I was able to have my two boys. I had to face many problems to become a mother, and the pain of losing your first child is miserable. That's one thing that when I talk about it, I get sensitive and very emotional because people don't understand what you are going through in your life. They always tend to judge others. There are a lot of women out there who cannot have a baby at all or are going through a lot of complications like I did.

Most often, when we women go out and face the world, every time we see somebody, they would ask, *"Do you have any children? Are you planning to have children?"* Especially when they have been married for a long time. That is one thing we have to stop because you don't know what that person is going through. You don't know how much they have been trying. Nobody knew what I was going through unless I told them. People would keep asking me, *"Are you going to stay with only one child?"* Sometimes I just wanted to say, *"Shut up!! Why do you keep asking me the same thing? You don't know what is going on with my life,"* but I could not. I just wanted to confine myself to home and never face the world.

That is why I say that we have to be more sensitive and we have to be more careful when we speak to others.

I did not stop working during my second pregnancy, although it was high-risk, especially because of the age factor. When I had my second baby, I was thirty-five years old, and I had my first child when I was twenty-four. It was risky due to many factors, but I was able to manage.

My checkup was different than a regular pregnant woman. Like if others needed to go to the hospital once, I needed to go twice a month. I had iron deficiency because my red blood cells were very low. Due to this, I became sluggish. I was always falling asleep everywhere. I used to fall asleep, even at work. I would be sitting watching TV, and all of a sudden, fall asleep. I was fatigued and low all the time.

Since my hemoglobin was very low, I went to a specialist for it. They did three transfusions so I would be able to deliver the baby without any complications. Thank God I was a strong woman and had a normal delivery. Even though I had a normal delivery, I had chances for C-section. However, by the grace and mercy of God, I was able to have my two babies normal and healthy. This is how another angel was born, Josiah Schmuel and it was a boy again. Both my sons have an age gap of almost eleven years. With my first child, they had to induce my labor, whereas, during my second child, they did not. However, I had to get the epidural for both of my deliveries because my condition was critical. I feel lot of pain during the process of having children was harrowing, but I am blessed.

I am happy, and I am thankful to God that I was able to have two boys that I wanted. It is not that I don't like females, I myself am one, besides the fact that I had to go through a lot throughout my life. I believe I am blessed to be surrounded by three men. I feel like I am a queen in the house, and I truly am. They treat me like one. I feel like the greatest mother. I give my children everything I can.

Of course, there are moments when I have to say, *"No, I am not going to be able to get it,"* but I work for them. I work very hard to be able to provide facilities for my children, to give them the best of education. They don't go to private school. They go to a public school. However, I, as a mother, try my best to give them whatever I can. I sit down with my children and talk about everything with them like how their day went by, help them with their homework, help them with their school projects, and play around with them like I am one of them. My oldest son is 19 years old now, and I act with him like we are age-mates. We play basketball; I taught him how to dance, and even how to dress in a fashionable manner. I taught my sons everything that I possibly could because I want them to be role models. I don't expect them to be perfect, but I just want people who see them wherever to say, *"What wonderful gentlemen Jocelyn has!"* I am not perfect; I make a lot of mistakes. I am a human, and so are my children, but I just want the best for them, but most of all, I want my kids to be happy.

Now when I look at my sons all beautifully grown up, I remember my mother's words that she said to me the night before she died. She said, *"You are going to be such a great mother!"* Her words never really left my mind. They always echoed in my head. I hope wherever she is, she can see that her words are a reality now, and I hope she is proud of me. Those words that she said to me have stuck with me throughout my life and made me the mother that I am today. It is one of the reasons why I wanted to be the best mother and to nurture the best of children. Despite all the hurdles and all that my husband and I went through, we were able to build a family. Believe me. It was hard. It was so ugly that I never want anyone to go through what I went through. All the sleepless nights, all the worst arguments at one point where we wanted to leave each other, all the mental pain that I had to bear, all of it feels like it was a dark and long night full of storms. God always has plans, and no matter how long the night is, it has to end. In the end, the dawn breaks, and the light that lifts up is always worth it.

Finally, I feel that the long dark night had come to an end, and everything was starting to make more sense. It was a peaceful, bright sunny morning of our life, and I just hoped for it last longer than the dark night.

Chapter 10
Lost Blood

Blood, if we think about it, it's nothing but just a liquid flowing through our veins. If we dig deeper, though, it is what makes humans related to each other and creates families. It is an integral part of how humans operate. You do not just share blood with your family, you share a bond, a connection, a relation of love and respect, that is what families are for. It is like different entities with different perceptions and different points of view getting united under one roof because of just one thing in common, the blood.

This chapter is very special and close to my heart because it is about my only brother. I am hoping you remember I mentioned in the initial chapters that when my mother died, my brother was just a baby. He was four years old while I was nine, and that is the time I became very close to him. I hope you remember the day my mother passed away, I held onto him and started running on the street holding him in my arms, until some relative found us and brought us back home. I loved him so much that I wanted to be just with him.

Then, time flew by, and life happened. Since my father was away most of the time due to work, he put my brother in charge of us sisters. Considering my brother was the only son, my father wanted him to take responsibility and be in charge when dad was not around. It was my brother who was responsible for protecting us at a very young age, when we were home alone, making sure no stranger enters our home, or we don't leave home without telling him.

My brother took his responsibilities too seriously, or maybe they got onto his nerves. He was always keeping his eyes on us, especially me, because we were close to each other. Although there were my older sister and my younger sister in the house, he was so attached to me that he would only pay attention to everything I did. Keep in mind my brother is the youngest.

In my teen life, I was very outgoing, and I am sure you must have gotten an idea by now. I used to go out with my friends without my father knowing, of course. However, since my brother was in charge, he would always drag himself in the way and say things like, *"I am not going to let anyone out*." But you know nothing was stopping me from partying with my friends, so I used to bribe my own brother.

As you remember, my father did not allow us to go out. Yes, I used to pay him to keep his mouth quiet, and not to let my father know that I went out with my friends. We had an age gap of almost five years, but we grew up together, we got very close to each other. We used to protect each other and keep each other's secrets. There were also times when we used to fight badly, but that did not change anything. This usually used to happen when my father was not around.

When my father came back home, he would always find out, nonetheless. One day we fought so bad that we broke a window in our apartment. It was me who broke it, and you would not be surprised to know that I took my brother and pushed him on the window so hard that it broke. I almost threw him out of it; that is how serious that fights were.

I don't know what used to get inside us, but our fights were horrible, and this is something I am not proud of. I remember we even used to hide each other's stuff when one of us told our father something the other did. We used to be so jealous of each other that we would act selfishly. We just wanted to beat each other for no reason. Of course, at the end of the day, we knew we will not ever hurt each other intentionally, but then again, we remembered none of it when we fought. As we got older and years passed by, the time for my marriage arrived. My brother was fourteen years old then, and I decided that I will not include him in my wedding. I had my reasons, and I knew he would only get protective. However, just before the wedding ceremony, my brother came up to me and said, *"If I am not a part of your wedding, I am going to destroy your dress the time when you are ready to walk down the aisle at church."* Laughter!

I got terrified, and my heart started to race. I was thinking to myself, 'Oh my God! He probably will destroy my dress.' I was frightened because everything he used to tell me that he would do something; he used to do it. That is why I believed everything he said to me. I had to find another pointer to point on him so that I could include him in my wedding.

Eventually, my brother made it to my wedding - I had to let him be part of it. After my marriage, my brother decided to move out for further studies, and we physically parted our ways. Deep down, however, I knew I loved him so much, and he loved me a lot too. It hurt me when he left, even though I was married. We still kept the relationship, but I don't know what happened to my brother. Years later, when my brother came back home from college, he created a family of his own, and things changed between us. Even though we used to communicate with each other, he became very much aggressive for some odd reason. It was like our communication was in total disagreement all the time. I tried to understand why this was happening but never really go to any conclusion.

The biggest issue was that he did not respect whatever I said or did. He used to get very aggressive against me, and I hated it. Unlike my brother, I am the type of person who respects others' opinions a lot. Even though I do not agree with everything people have to say or believe, but I don't get aggressive about it, well unless you get me to that breaking point. I will directly tell the other person I don't agree with them, and I will find a way to say it very nicely, but some people don't know that tactic, and my brother was one of them in my eyes.

I still don't understand why, but my brother's anger was uncontrollable. Sometimes, we used to fight over dumb things. He would approach me and tell me that what I did or am doing is wrong. I admit that being a brother, he had all the rights to tell me where I went wrong, but he never correctly did that. So, I used to get very upset and argue back with him. He would get so rude and rough that at the end of arguments that I would just prefer cutting him off. Now, I am not the type of person who would never cut someone out for just any reason, but in my brother's case, I had to do it. Everyone has their limits, so do I. He made me get to that point where I got agitated and lost it, and when I lose my temperament, I start to curse. I mentioned in the previous chapters that all my siblings have Gardner's Syndrome except for me. I am not sure if this attitude is because he is ill, but he was irritable. There was a point where he told me that I did not understand what he was going through because I am not sick, and I don't have the condition.

That hurt me a lot because I felt desperate for them, and I was the one who spent months studying that disease so that I could help my family heal. I still was always the person present at the hospital whenever he goes for any major procedures, even if I am not talking to him. Nonetheless, I think it was not a right thing to do either because as long as he used to be in the hospital, we used to get normal with each other, and as soon as he was better and got out of the hospital, we would start arguing again and cut each other off. Most of the time, when we argued, I used to cry badly and hang up on him. I told him that he was the one who did not understand me. I would ask him, *"Why do you do this to me?"* but he always acted like he did not do anything. He would justify it by saying, "You are dramatic. You are overwhelmed; that is why you are crying, and it's not about me."

I used to sit on my bed and wonder why he acted the way he did. Is it my fault that I don't have that disease? Is it my fault that we could never be the siblings we could have been? Then again, I think about how it is not my fault that he always calls me and says all these mean things to me? All I used to do is protect myself against him because of the things that he says to me.

At some point, I started thinking that my brother was annoyed with my existence. I couldn't understand his behaviors towards me. However, I said no one should have a competition with anyone because we all are capable of achieving whatever we want if we put our minds into it.

Words cut deeper than a knife, which is why I always say that we have to look out for what we say to each other and think twice before uttering a word. We should always wonder why we say something to someone. My brother should also have thought this way when he said that I had become overwhelming, and he does not do anything to me. Even if he thought so, he should have been concerned as to why I was so stressed out or behaving a certain way. It is rude to pass remarks and not be able to justify or help another with that –, is not it? I always emphasize asking questions like 'why did I say to this to him or her?', 'was it necessary?', 'why did I have to make her feel so horrible that she is crying?' Nonetheless, my brother never really cared about the things he said to me, this is what I believe.

I am sure there are siblings out there and families who are going through the same phase, probably arguing or fighting for no reason. To all of you reading this, believe me, it is the worst thing to do. A family should always stay united no matter how many storms they have to survive. We, as a family, should always be able to sit on one table and laugh. We should be able to talk about things with each other and comfort each other. We should avoid getting into arguments for no reason, and if we do, resolve and move on.

There was a point in my life when my brother and I did not talk for months. The things that he had said to me hurt me so much that I chose to walk away from him, and he also chose to walk away from me. That is when I decided that I will not let him hurt me anymore, and I decided to get order protection against him. His words to me were no less than harassment. I was sure about getting order protection to stop him from passing near the place I lived or even the neighborhood. I just did not want to see his face, and it was equally painful for me. We grew up together, taking care of each other, and look at us now.

I always thought that having a brother is like having a best friend, but we lost that connection. Although we have an age-gap of years, I used to believe that having a brother is like having a protector - somebody I can count on, somebody that I can call whenever in need, someone who can guide me, and I can guide him.

He can say to me that, *"Okay, you did this, but what I think is you should do this,"* and at the same time respect each other. I guess it was because my father gave him the authority when he was small, and he took advantage of it. He thought he could do whatever he wants to do and treat me the way he wants; however, I don't think that was right in any way. My brother's behavior towards me was affecting my mental and physical health, and I felt he was abusing me emotionally.

I got so depressed that I was going to see a doctor because I could not sleep at night. My situation got so bad that I used to shiver hearing my brother's name, especially around the time when we used to argue. I used to call his wife and say, *"I am going to put order protection against him. I don't want him near me, I don't want him to talk to me, and I don't want to know anything about him. I want the best for him, I know who my brother is, and I love him more than anything. But I would rather separate myself from him, depart from him to live a good life because he is affecting my health. I am taking medication to be able to go to sleep because that's how bad things were emotionally affecting me."*

I actually wanted to get order protection against him, but I never really got it. The reason behind this is that when my father found out about it, he was so hurt to know that our relationship had only worsened over time. I felt bad for my father and believed that we are going to end up in something ugly, so I decided not to do it. Nevertheless, I also know that my father used to talk to him about it. He wanted to counsel him, but he failed. Our father wanted us to stop arguing and be united again. Now that I am a mother and I think about it, it is ugly how we used to love each other and still argue. I can feel how our father must have been feeling for years. It makes no sense to argue with your siblings as we did. I know this happens in every family or most of the families, but now that I am older, having children of my own, I don't want them to go through that. I regret that we had to go through that.

One thing I have to say is, thanks to my younger sister. She was always supporting me and always supported who was right. I am so thankful she is always around and tries to keep us united, but it did not work. My father always would have wanted us to be united and to avoid unnecessary arguments. I know our arguments used to affect my father too because sometimes we used to argue in front of him.

Sometimes the argument used to get so heated up that I used to say to my brother, *"Get out of my house."* No father would like to witness his children arguing like cats and dogs, so dad, this is for you: I am sorry; we are sorry! I really want us to reconcile. I want us to forget about the past and say to him, *"Let's be the best brother and sister again like we were as children."* We used to go out together everywhere. We talked to each other and played so many games, helped each other with homework, and even dressed alike sometimes. I miss that time and childhood, indeed. It was the most beautiful part of our life. Talking about childhood, I cannot help but think about my mother, she must have been so disappointed watching us fight from above.

That is another reason why I want me and my brother to be able to get back to how we were as children. We loved each other so much. Life is getting short, and we are getting closer to death every single day. I want us to be able to hug each other before it ends, and never hold a grudge against each other, which I already don't. I don't hold anything against him. I don't forget, but I forgive very easily. It is just that I miss him a lot; I miss our complete family.

I want to dedicate this chapter of my book to my only brother, to set an example for his children and his grandchildren. I want them to read this, so when we both leave this world, they can say their father was a great man, which I know he is to his children. One piece of advice I must say, how can you say to your children, especially when they have brothers too, that you have to be good to your sister when you have not set that example yourself for them to follow? This goes to you. Whenever you read this part, I want you to know that I love you so much. I chose to write this here because I want you to understand how much you hurt me even though you think you did not. You hurt me with your words, with your behavior towards my family and me. I know I am not perfect; I know I make mistakes, and I probably hurt you too, but we have to stop that right here. Life is short, and we never know what is going to happen in the next moment. The versions that we are today is a shame for both of us, especially the way we grew up, we should not be having arguments just because.

I want to make my father proud. I want him to notice that we, as brother and sister, we loved each other, and we can become the best brothers and sisters in the world. I hope that we can reconcile, and we can forget about the past and leave an example for our children that brothers and sisters must love each other, no matter what. We have to respect each other and each other's opinion knowing that we both see the world differently.

It's ok that you if tell me what you think and you have the right to do so, but you should also have to respect what I decided to do anyway because I am not a child. I am a grown-up woman, and I have my own decisions to make. Being that I am the oldest sister, you need to respect me as I respect you, and I don't argue with you about the decisions you make. I don't stop you; I advise you. I just say that *"I don't think you should do this,"* but if you do it anyway, it's your choice, and I respect that. At the end of the day, it's your decision about how you want to live your life. That is what I want to teach our children, and whoever reads this book, 'learn to respect each other's choices.'

This particular chapter is very special to me because I confess how our relationship is and want to have a good relationship with him again. I don't want to die. But if I do and we never resolve our relationship. I just want you to know. I wanted to have a brother that I can call a best friend. That I can tell the world this is my brother, the one that despite all the facts I am proud of. I am proud of my brother. I tell everybody that he is my brother, but he is not the brother that I always dreamed of having. It is hard when you are walking to a place, and you know your brother is sitting there, and you just walk like he was not there. It was tough for me. So, I want my brother to know I never want to relive that day, and I want things to be better between us.

Just remember if you are reading this, this chapter is for you to stop. Don't do this. I am your sister, the one you once loved so much. Siblings don't even remember how they started arguments, but they keep claiming just for the sake of ego. It prevents them from being humble and admitting that they did wrong. I know you would never admit you were wrong. I also understand that siblings do argue, but don't let it be the reason for becoming strangers to each other. I will always love you, and I can never stop loving you because you are my only brother and because you are my blood.

Besides the fact that we argue, I hope one day we get back to being normal and become the best buddies ever. It breaks my heart to think that I could not maintain an ideal relationship with my one and only brother. Especially, now that the family has shrunk and there are not many people left.

In the end, I request you (my brother) to please let the past be in the past and let the bygone be bygone. Let's collect the broken pieces and stick them together. I hope you will understand my reasons and the way I behaved. All I have to say is that despite everything, you still mean a lot to me. It's time we make peace and be the family we were always meant to be. I know things are not easy in your life, and you also have been going through a lot of hardship. Though remember that we share the same blood, and we belong together. No matter how much we run far away from each other, the universe will always push us back together. This time, let it not be the universe but our own hearts that pull us back together. Let's just hug each other before the time slips out of our hands…

"Like branches on a tree, we grow in different directions, yet our roots remain as one. Each of our lives will always be a special part of the other."

-Unknown

Chapter 11
Dear Sister

Sisters are the first best friends we make as kids without even knowing the meaning of friendship. We laugh together, we tease each other, we make mistakes, we wipe each other's tears, we are ever ready to fight for them, and our love for them is unconditional. The oldest sister is usually the one who plays the role of a guardian, supporter and helper, the one you look up to after your mother, and the one who gives you the right advice always.

My oldest sister and I shared a similar relation. She became my best friend, my mother, my everything after my mother passed away. She took care of me at every step of life and made sure my younger sister and I had everything I needed despite the fact she was sick.

Unfortunately, she was going through the same condition as our mother, and I have to say that it is horrible to see someone going through it at such a young age. It was heartbreaking, but just like my mother, she was such a strong woman that she never let anyone feel how painful it was. She taught me a lot of things. Even through severe sickness, she had so much courage to take care of her only child. She was very protective when it came to him since he was everything to her. The disease was eating her alive little by little; it was destroying her, and it saddened me, but she never let it come between her responsibilities towards her child.

If we talk about her personality, my sister was a social butterfly. Her personality was so charming that everyone in a room noticed her wherever she went. That is how strong her soul was, but looking at her son was the only thing that made her weak. Even the terrible disease that had gotten to her could not weaken her, but her son easily could. Watching such a social human lying on bed, helpless, was heart-wrenching.

Dear sister, I recall when you were lying on the bed, too sick to even move an inch. You were only worried about your son and his upbringing. You were so scared to leave the world, not because of yourself but because you did not know what is going to happen to him. You would tell our younger sister and me that, *"I want you to take care of him,"* and then we used to argue with our younger sister. You were back and forth between the younger sister and myself. She would insist that she wanted that responsibility, and I used to come back to me and say that, *"You need to take care of him when I am not around, and if I ever leave, you are responsible for him."* It was like a continuous argument between us. I was worried about who was going to take care of my nephew and who was going to stay with him.

Dear sister, there is one thing that I can never forget. It was when you finally decided between your two sisters; me and the younger one, as to who was going to take the custody of your child. It was then I knew how much you loved and trusted me. You picked me for the huge and important responsibility; you picked my husband and me to take care of your child. You even decided to call the priest and arrange a baptism so that we can also become the child's godparents.

Fulfilling what you wished, we called a priest to the house and did a small baptism ceremony. I became my nephew's godmother, and my husband became his godfather. I will never forget when you used to say, *"I want you guys to take care of him. I know that he is going to be in good hands, and I know you and your husband are going to be the ideal mother and the father I want my child to have when I am not here in this world."*

Although you were satisfied and content with the decision you made, you were also worried about the chances of your son inheriting the disease too. You wanted to ensure that your child does not have the condition which was taking your life away. That is when you made a decision that you want him to be taken to the hospital and get checked. It was not just you; we were all so scared about it because we were afraid that he was going to have the condition that you had.

The appointment was made for your son to be checked, and we were all hoping for a miracle. He was only twelve years old then. He was entering puberty, so it was a perfect time to check if he had the disease. The doctors did the tests, and oh my God!! I was so surprised to hear the results. The thing we were so scared of had turned out to be true. My nephew, your only son, had inherited the condition that you, my sister, was dying of, and it was horrible.

You left your son with not only us but also the condition that came from my mother. Right away, the doctors said, *"Although he is very young, his intestine has a lot of polyps already."* His condition was becoming very aggressive; therefore, the doctors decided to remove a part of his colon at that age.

Therefore, when my nephew was only twelve years old, they removed a part of his colon, they did a sub-total removal of his Colon. He was in the hospital for a week or two. My younger sister and I were taking turns to stay at the hospital with our nephew. On the other hand, my oldest sister, the child's mom, was bed-ridden. She was very ill.

My nephew got his surgery around February 2003. He came back home, and the process of recovery began. Since he was young, he did not pay much attention to anything. He just knew that he was going to have surgery and that he was sick. He was not concerned about what was going on with him, but he knew that he inherited his mother's condition.

Even after finding out her son had the same disease, my sister remained patient. That is one thing that helped me become a brave woman and a stronger mother. I saw my sister as my ideal. She made sure that before she leaves this world, her son was in the safest hands. She knew her condition was only getting worse. Therefore, she made sure he was well taken care of, and there was someone to keep a check on him. He was sick, so she wanted someone to be there to take care of him and keep check of all his medical appointments and pills.

A lot happened during that time of my life. My sister's condition was rapidly worsening. During that time, I also decided to change myself a little bit. I used to have big breasts. My breasts were a bit big as compared to my body. I was small, just a hundred pounds, and my breasts were a little big for myself due to which I was getting a lot of back and shoulder pain. I was going for therapy, but nothing was helping me.

I remember when I told you, dear sister, that I was going to do breast reduction, you were in a semi-coma.

My sister was only in her late twenties, and she went through so many surgeries. By this time, anybody who used to mention any kind of surgery to her, she used to go like, *"Don't do it if you don't have to or until it is medically recommended and really needed."* Therefore, when I told her that I wanted to reduce my breast because it was affecting my health, she was not so happy about it because she said she loved the way that I looked and that I looked so perfect with my big breast. However, it was not about the looks only. I was in pain, and therapies were not helping me. Therefore, the doctor decided to recommend surgery, and I did it despite my sister's disagreement and my husband's.

When I got admitted to the hospital, it was such a weird feeling. Many fears were taking over my head. What if the surgery did not go right? What if I have to stay in the hospital longer? What if something happened to my sister while I got my surgery done? I could feel how my sister must have been feeling lying on that hospital bed for so long. I can never forget that the day I was supposed to get the surgery, my sister went into a coma.

I was scared not because of the surgery, but because I dreaded something happening to my sister in the meantime. I wanted her to see me and to see the difference in myself before and after the surgery. I wanted her to feel that regardless of what I do to my body, I am still going to be her sister, and my soul is still going to be the same.

I got done with it, and fortunately, everything came out well after the surgery. I wanted my sister to see me the way I looked, so I went to her straight away. When my sister came out of the coma a few days later, she said: *"You look okay, but I liked the other Jocelyn more with the big breasts and sexy looks."* I can never forget what I replied to her. I said, *"I am still going to be the same, even though I look a little bit weird. Once you get used to how I look now, it will be fine."* I remember telling her, *"For now, give me a big hug because you are going to feel me closer now."* She just smiled at me; she was kind of on and off from the coma. My sister was in the house because she was already under Hospice at home. She signed her DNR papers that said, 'Do not Resuscitate.' We had it against her bed on the wall. She was well-equipped at home, with a hospital bed, an oxygen tank, and all you can imagine a sick person could have. All family members use to come around to see my sister, and everyone was very supportive.

My sister was a brave woman. I know it is hard to believe, but she used to call me in her room and even pre-arranged her funeral. She told me what she wanted at her funeral, how she wanted to be dressed, and even what color she wanted to wear. She wanted red roses and wished to wear white because she never got married. She did not want a fancy dress; she wanted to look sophisticated, very special, but elegant at the same time. She even told me how she wanted her hair to be done. My sister also wanted the music to be played at her funeral. Of course, the music was really sad. The music that she picked for her funeral was saying good-bye to all of us and telling us how life is full of surprises. It was about how you don't live forever, and that the only thing that lasts is eternity. Even though my sister did not know what eternity was because she was still alive, she felt the peace associated with it. She knew that it is the only thing that lasts forever, but she was also of the opinion that we must appreciate life and enjoy it while we can because we never know what is going to happen to us the next moment.

Whenever my sister pulled me in her room to tell me all these things, I used to breakdown and cry. I used to tell her, *"Please don't tell these things to me because I hope that one day you will get up from the bed, and you are going to survive."*

However, she was reluctant to accept any of those consolations and said, *"This is my reality, and I want you to hear me. At least you can fulfill my wish to arrange my funeral the way I want."* I said to her, *"Give me the money! You are asking for all these things, but where is the money to get them done?"* I said it on the lighter note, of course, and we always broke out laughing. She used to say, *"I want you to be happier. Always be happy, but don't separate yourself from my son. Always take care of him and make sure he is okay, and I want you to make sure that he is fine."*

Whenever we used to have that conversation, my younger sister used to get a little obsessed because I used to breakdown. My elder sister was so funny that she used to tell my younger sister, *"Let her cry! Let her cry in front of me because when I die, I will not be able to see her crying."* She was too much. She was full of life but also depressed because of her condition.

As a mother, my older sister was very protective towards her child, so much so that sometimes I used to bluntly say to her, *"Stop behaving like that because if you pass away, I will be left with your spoiled child. What am I going to do when you are not here? He is going to miss you so badly, and he will not listen to me. So, you have to be a little bit more laid back and let me correct him if I have to. Don't feel that I am doing it out of responsibility. I am doing it because I want the best for him, and if he is doing something wrong, I have to correct him."* None of that stopped her, of course. She was so protective of him that she did not want anyone to make him feel bad or say anything to her child. She wanted to pamper him as much as she could because she knew she was eventually going to leave him.

The day that we all dreaded the most did come, and it was ugly. I always used to say to my youngest sister and to myself that whenever my sister dies, I wouldn't want to be anywhere around her because I did not know how I was going to react. I could not see her taking her last breath. I recall the days my sister got so sick that she was not able to walk anymore. She was surviving on constant oxygen and could barely breathe. That was my biggest fear that I saw in my head; I used to think that my sister is going to die gasping for air because she could not breathe.

It was so because she was always asking, *"Can you make the oxygen levels higher because I cannot breathe."* She was in a lot of pain, and I could not see her that way. We could not even touch her skin. She felt pain everywhere in her body. The cancer spread, and it went all over her body. I hope you remember that I mentioned that Gardner's Syndrome eventually becomes cancerous because of the type of tumors that you get if you are able to survive until the end. Some people don't get cancer but die of other complications due to the condition as well. The day that my sister died was May 29, 2003. That day I went to work, but I left work early because my sister's home health aide had a medical appointment. She asked me if I could go with her to help her with the translation. I got to my elder sister's home. I did not go upstairs to see her; I just took the car service and went to pick up her caretaker. When I picked her up, I asked her how my sister was doing. She was already in a coma or agonizing, and she was not talking anymore. She was just breathing with the help of the oxygen machine. We just used to touch her; I touched her to make her feel her let her know we were there.

I recall my sister telling me in a very low voice, *"I will not leave this world until you say to me that you are going to take care of my son. Say that you are going to make sure that he is going to be fine and that you are going to keep him with you and our family."* She wanted me to promise her that he is not going to go anywhere and is going to stay with me and all of us, including my father. Therefore, I said to my sister not to worry about it and that her son is going to be in good hands. I promised her that I was going to keep him around us, and he is not going to go anywhere. It was three days later when I took the car service, and I did not go upstairs. It's so strange because when we got to the hospital, besides that we were inches from the office, I felt pain in my heart and it was to the extent that I felt I was getting a heart attack. I held my chest, and I told my sister's caretaker, *"Oh my God! I am feeling so much pain. This pain is suffocating me."* Moments later, the pain disappeared. The caretaker's phone was constantly ringing. When her phone rang for the tenth time, she picked it up, and the only thing she said was, *"Okay, we are going there soon."*

I asked her right away, *"Please say that my sister is okay. Please don't tell me she passed away."* She said, *"No, no, they are going to take her to the hospital."* She did not want to tell me what had happened because of the sharp pain I had in my heart prior. I guessed that she was not letting me know that my sister is gone. When we got to the medical appointment, we went inside, and the caretaker asked if we could see the doctor right away. We were told the doctor had an emergency and she was going to be late. We found the doctor in the hallway, and she said, *"I have to go. You can reschedule your appointment."* So that's what we did.

When we got to my father's house, there was a police car outside. Here, I will reiterate that my sister was under Hospice care, and when you are under Hospice care, you don't go to the hospital. You call the doctor to the premises to treat patients instead. Even though I knew what had happened, I was still hoping that I was wrong. When I got to the house and saw the police car outside our home, my heart sank. I asked my uncle, who was outside, *"What's going on?"* He did not answer me and just told me to go upstairs. When I went upstairs with am pounding heart, the policeman was standing near the kitchen. It turned out my sister died in the house. She wanted to be home and died in her room in peace and around her family when nobody was really bothering her. Her wish was fulfilled.

When I walked into the room and saw my sister, I froze for a while. My eyes filled with tears; she was pale and not breathing anymore. I just dropped myself on the bed beside her and started crying. I was shouting, "*Don't leave me! Please don't leave me!"* but she was long gone. She looked so much in peace. She looked like a bird, declaring that she was finally free.

Later I found out that my father took my sister off the bed and helped her to the wheelchair. He gave her a natural juice to drink, and she drank it all. The juice was red, which made her mouth so red that you could almost mistake it for blood. She was alive then, but that did not last for long.

My father, my nephew, and my sister in law were there with my sister before her passing. I can recall my father saying, "When I was at work, something was telling me that I needed to go to the house." He could not work properly that day. He rushed to the house before my sister passed. He took her off the bed because he had so much hope that she was going to wake up and is going to be back to be normal.

I did not pre-arrange my sister's funeral because I believe it should only be done when the person is no longer here. Now that she was gone, I called my husband and told him what happened. As broken as I was, I don't know where I got all this strength from. My heart was in pieces; I felt like somebody just took a hammer and smashed my heart down. Nobody was in the condition to arrange anything, but I had to fulfill her last wishes.

My husband and I took responsibility. I asked him to call the funeral home and arrange everything she had wanted to be done for her funeral. I asked him to pre-arrange everything right away. A lot of family members came over, and they were all crying. Even if you know a family member is very sick, even if you know they are going to die, no matter how much you think prepared you are, you are not. You never want that moment to come. You are never prepared beforehand, especially for the loss of a close family member. To me, my sister was more than just an elder sibling. I not only loved her like my sister but like my second mother because when my mother died, I grew up with her. She took care of me, and we were also best friends. She was four years older than me. She died at the very young age of twenty-nine. She looked so calm and young; her skin had become so smooth. The transformation of dying made her look as if she was not more than twenty years old. It looked as if all her sickness was erased from her body and her face. Nobody could believe that she was sick for so many years.

When the time for the funeral came, it was so devastating because they took her body and put it in a black bag. Even though they do it very nicely, I just could not. We all hid in a room and covered ourselves to avoid seeing them taking my sister away. It was so harsh. She was bed-bound for so many years and could not come out of the house at all. The only time I used to see her was when she was lying down in bed or coming to the living room in her wheelchair. It was devastating to see such a young person going through that. Now when she was finally going out of the house, it was death in a bag. Moreover, everything was arranged for the funeral the way my sisters wished for it. It was just the way she wanted or even better. I recall my father; he was so upset because my younger sister and I went crazy looking for the clothes she wanted and let the funeral person know how she wanted her hair to be done. Besides that, when she was dying, she asked me to do her makeup. She was so funny that she said, *"I want you to do my makeup because the funeral people make you look deader than how you are. They put so much makeup on you because they don't know how you were as a person when you were alive. They don't know how to fix you."* So, she assigned this task to me. This ignited yet another argument between my younger sister and me.

My older sister and I did not discuss the kind of makeup she wanted, but I was so brave that I did her makeup, and it came out so beautiful. She looked like a singer. Everyone who came to the funeral and saw her took a picture of her because she looked so beautiful. She looked just like a sleeping beauty. We also played music and everything she had asked before she died. Now, if we recall the beginning of this book when my mother had died, the three of us sisters were told that we were not supposed to show our emotions, we were not supposed to cry. It had left a significant impact on our lives. I still could not cry, thinking of what she had said to us. I wanted to scream so much because my sister died, but I was holding everything inside. I recall leaning on my sister's cascade, sitting on the little bench they usually put in front of the cascade. I was silently crying because I did not want anyone to know. I ended up having a panic attack. One of my uncles was there, who is a doctor, and he assured everyone that I was fine. I just had a panic attack, so they gave me water to drink to calm me down. I could not breathe because I wanted to scream, but I was trained to keep it all inside.

My life turned into black and white again; I could see no colors. After my sister died, I suffered panic attacks and developed anxiety. When I have to wait too long for something, I get panicked. I start developing anxiety. I developed the fear of losing someone. Even today, if I make new friends or I get too close to someone, and that person stops being a part of my life, I develop a lot of anxiety. I have been trying to control it. Sometimes I take medications for it, but I try to stay away from it because I want to live my life in reality. I don't want to be dropped out, not knowing what's going on around me. I am very expressive about my feelings, and if I feel something towards somebody, I will be the first person to tell them about any situation. Therefore, it was hard for me. Now we were left with my nephew, and so it was a lot of things to work on. My nephew fell sick very badly after my sister died. He was not speaking to anyone, so I was constantly running to the psychologists, trying to cope with the situation. Since I had been in that situation, I knew how it felt. In my heart, I just knew I would do everything I can for him. I became my nephew's legal guardian. So, every doctor's appointment that he had, I was there with him. I was taking care of his school, making sure he goes to school regularly.

So, dear sister, you should be happy that you left your son with us. We took great care of him, and our younger sister also played a huge role in his wellbeing. Our father and just about everyone played a big part as well. I have to tell you that you made the best choice to leave him with us. We tried our very best to help him, guide him, and put him on the right path in his life. He is thirty years old now. He is still struggling with the condition but is very stable. He is married with one child. His wife make sure he goes to his medical appointments regularly. I fulfilled every promise I made to you. This condition is not a joke; every time a person goes to a medical appointment with this condition, they never get good news. There is a piece of bad news or another. Sometimes, everything can be stable, but other times, it's not, and this is a known fact. My sister picked me to be the person who takes care of her son, and that's what I tried to do best.

Losing my sister was hard. There came the point when I got so depressed that I wanted to kill myself and my son as well because I did not want to leave him behind. I got very emotional because it is hard to lose two people who are both motherly-figures to you. I did not want to live, but I also did not want to leave my son behind. My son was one and a half years old, and I know well the pain of not having a mother at such an early age, even though I had such a great father by my side.

I did not say anything to anyone, but I guess God touched my heart and told me that don't do what you are planning to do because it is going to be devastating for your father and the entire family. I was planning. I told my father and my husband that I don't want to live anymore. I told them that I am going to kill myself and the baby. They were so shocked to hear this. They went crazy. In the end, thank God they helped me get over it. Nonetheless, I had to let it out somewhere else, so I became an alcoholic. It was as if whoever is too close to me; God steals them from me. I started drinking nonstop because I wanted my sister back. I knew it was not possible, but I was selfish with myself. I was just drinking even in the house, knowing I had a baby and a job that I was responsible for. My routine involved going to work, coming back to the baby, and drinking relentlessly. Then I realized that I needed to stop drinking because I had a lot to take care of. I ruralized. I was not hurting anyone but myself. I had another sister and a child who needed me.

I had my husband to help me cope with my grief, but either way, it is not easy to lose someone close. That is why I always encourage everyone to express the love for the ones you want in your life, be the best you can with them, respect each other, and communicate. If you think you cannot be nice to someday, just walk away. If it is important to you, try to make that relationship work because that's life. You never know what is going to happen to any of us. For me, it happened too often, and always unexpectedly. You are not even sure about the next moment, so always be nice to everyone. I learned a lot from adversity, and it had a huge impact on my life. Dear sister, you were one of the best people I came across in this lifetime. I learned from you how to be a good mother, how to protect my child, and how to take care of your child along with mine. But one thing I learned from you was to always love myself. While you were alive, I learned how good it is to have another mother when your mother is no more.

That's one thing I will appreciate all my life. I know one day we are going to see each other again. I am going to be able to hug you and tell you how much I love you. No matter how old I get, I will always miss you and feel your absence in my life. No one can ever replace you in my heart. The lessons I learned, all the love and warmth you gave me without even asking, I will be forever thankful for that.

I just have one regret, and that is that all of this did not last long. You left me too soon. I miss that warmth; I feel cold and numb. A piece of my heart is missing, and nothing in this world can ever make me feel full again. I am empty on the inside, but I cannot just do anything that could bring you back. I just pray for you. I pray that wherever you are, you are free and in peace, without any pain, and you are happy watching over your son and us.

It is not easy; it never was, and I badly miss the other part of me that was you.

"If you have a sister and she dies, do you stop saying you have one? Or are you always a sister, even when the other half of the equation is gone?"

-Jodi Picoult

Chapter 12
My Career

Every person in this world has a dream, a goal that they want to accomplish. As kids, we say, 'I want to be a pilot when I grow up,' but when we grow up and open our eyes to the real world, we realize that becoming a pilot is not what we want at all. Everyone wants to be successful; nobody wants to be left behind. Some want to be a doctor, some want to be an engineer, some dream of opting for Air Force as their career, but I, well, my destiny had a different plan for me, and I do not regret a bit of who I am today. I strongly believe in making myself better as a person and as a professional, no matter what field I work in.

Back in 1995, when I decided to go back to college after my marriage, I think it was the best decision that I ever made. I was very young and passionate. I had big dreams and a lot of careers to pick from. To be honest, I did not know what I wanted to do, but one thing that I was sure about was that I wanted to have the opportunity to become a professional and to learn countless new things. However, the fact that I was confused about what I wanted to do remains.

There was only one thing that I was very passionate about; it was doing my own business to learn how to work in the world of business. Therefore, it made it easier for me to pick my majors. I chose business and accounting as my majors because I love mathematics. I get fascinated by playing with numbers. Even though I love writing because that is how I express myself, I was not choosing it as a career or a field in which I have to write a lot.

I guess it was because I was pretty much doing it all my life. Hence, I picked the numbers. It was not easy. My majors had to do a lot with factors. It was also the time when my sister was very sick. A lot of things were happening. Things were getting very hard for me. My routine involved running back and forth between personal and professional life, concentrating on studies, and working at the same time.

Despite everything, I was trying my best to balance out everything, but my GPA was quite low during that time. It was getting tough, but I said to myself that I am not going to give up. I was determined to push myself forward, and I am increasing my GPA. I decided to work very hard. I used to tell myself that I know it's not easy, I know it's going to take time, but I have to find myself to do better. I am the type of person who never gives up easily. So, when I decide to do something, I could be scared in the beginning, I could be scared in the middle of what I am doing, but giving up is not an option for me. In spite of all the hardships, I said to myself, "I am going to continue regardless of whatever is going on in my life, and I am going to push myself to do the best." It was overwhelming; I was working a part-time job.

I had just got married practically, which was back in 1995, but believe it or not, my husband was one of the rare persons who pushed me to go to college and to improve myself and to become a professional. I did not want to disappoint him; I continued to push myself to work and learn business and accounting, while at the same time involving myself in my sister's sickness and work.

I worked hard on myself. Every time I saw an opportunity to grow, I was the first one there learning, I never said no to anything. I believe in grabbing any opportunity that you get on your way to your final destination. Grasp it, and don't let go! Don't miss that opportunity because it is never going to come back again. In certain cases, we might say no because we think it is not a part of our job, and we may regret it later. I think that attitude is wrong. You should go for it because you should learn when you are given a chance to. Make the most out of the opportunity that is given to you. That is one thing I always had in my mind; to continue to grow and learn and never quit. Though I had the support of my husband, I was very much self-motivated, always pushing myself forward, encouraging, and supporting my own self, encouraging myself never to give up.

Another big supporter that I had when I was going to school and college was my father, my hero. Every girl sees her father as an ideal man, and so did I. He was such an amazing supporter to me and my sisters. He was also always encouraging me to go to school; in fact, my younger sister, too, since she was going to high-school at the same time I was. Though she was going into a different career, we were both there, trying to better ourselves. It was equally hard for both of us, but we did our best to be there.

When I was in college, I also used to help our assistant director. If she needed anything, or if there was an activity or program in college, I was the first one to participate. If there was anything related to work, or anything that they had that I believed I could learn from it, I used to get involved. I believe learning is a mighty weapon. When you have a lot of knowledge and keep learning, you grow in ways you never even imagined. That is why I never missed a single opportunity to learn something new and grow. This is one of the reasons why I like to share my ideas and whatever I learn. I don't like to keep the knowledge to myself. I feel its injustice to others and myself. I feel good when people learn from what I learned.

That is one more fact about me; if I know something, I will not be selfish with it and share it with you. I am not afraid that if I give you the information, you might have my job. I don't care. I like to give out the information as much as I can, especially when I know it is going to be beneficial for the other person and something they could learn from. Also, keep in mind that yes, there is some confidential information that I won't be able to share.

There came the point in time when going to college became really tough for me due to the workload. There were a lot of times when I wanted to quit; in fact, I skipped one semester because I was so overwhelmed. I needed a break for myself. Finally, after all that I survived, the big day came. I am not talking about my marriage or the day my baby was born; of course, those are important events for me, but this one was the closest to my heart because I had worked hard for it. It was the summer of the year 1999, the year I graduated. It was the best feeling. When I got the news that I was going to get graduated, I was jumping out of joy. I remember my college did a big celebration in one beautiful place and my whole family and I was oh-so-excited. At my prom party at the college or the celebration that they had, I don't remember what they called it at the time. I invited my aunts with their husbands, my sisters, and my brother.

My father could not make it because he had to stay with my nephew. The rest of us had a blast. It was so nice. Everybody was there, including my friends and family. We were all celebrating the news of my graduation. We went through so many things together, and seeing everyone happy, at least for a while, had me in tears. Hence, I was the first one to graduate at the time from the second generation.

The thing that made me the happiest was that even though my oldest sister was so sick at that time, she dressed beautifully to be there with me and to celebrate that I was graduating from college. I was so emotional and in disbelief that she was there. When I hugged her, she said to me, *"I am so proud of you, and I am so glad that you are graduating. I am happy that the college threw a party, and I am here celebrating with you and the rest of the family."* It was so nice for everyone to be there, celebrating that day.

It was something that I can never forget. The support of my family is something that I am so grateful for. There were ups and downs, but that is something that is in our lifeline. If the screen shows just a flat line without any bumps, a person is considered dead. So, these bumps are just part and parcel of life.

The time when I was going to college, I was already working in a company as an accountant assistant. It was a department store where they sell all kinds of stuff; it was like what we call a general department store. When I started working in that company, my first designation was a cashier. As I said before, I am the kind of person that likes to move forward, so I kept looking for better opportunities.

Coincidently, the company that I was working in had an opening to work in the corporate office as an accountant assistant, at the same time I was going to college. I thought to myself that it is the best opportunity for me to go for it. I went for the interview, and they gave me the job as a part-time, which was most suitable for me. By the time I graduated, I had learned so much already because of the hands-on experience I had got. I got more fascinated with the accounting, with the numbers, and doing all the transactions and everything that involved accounting. It was such a great experience. The day of the graduation ceremony came. I forgot the name of the place where they did it, but I was so excited. My husband, brother, and father accompanied me for the celebration because colleges only give you limited tickets for these types of celebrations. I had three tickets; thus, I picked my father, of course, my brother, and my husband.

It was such a wonderful day full of emotions and excitement, but I cannot deny how I missed my mother so much. I wished she was there to see me graduate, even after getting married. I knew she must be so proud looking at me from heaven above, so I was satisfied. I graduated from college and finally got to throw my hat to the sky like everyone else was doing. In short, it was a fantastic day.

I remember the celebration did not end even after coming back to home. We threw a big party with my sisters and my aunts. I can never forget that day; it was one of the rare days where I felt nothing but complete happiness. It was back in

1999, and it has been twenty-one years since I graduated from college. It has been a lot of years already, but it feels like yesterday. Furthermore, I decided to go back to college after I graduate to continue with my studies. However, I decided to take a break from everything, but then, during that break, I became pregnant again. It was yet another challenge for me, but I still went back to college. It was my second pregnancy, and I said to myself that I have to do what I have to do, and I am not going to give up. It was a great experience to return to college while I was pregnant, especially when it was something fruitful for me and something, I was passionate about.

A fact about life is that you never know what is going to happen next in yours. Sometimes you opt for some field, and you end up in some other. You just have to go with the flow. After 911, I decided to take the police officer test to join the police force. Everything went well, and I passed the test. However, for some odd reason, I changed my mind. When I was called, I decided to refuse to enter the academy. I guess because God had an even better plan for me. When my sister passed away in the year 2003, I was hired to work in a hospital in Brooklyn. Again, I was working as an assistant, helping with the accounting and anything that had to do with accounting. Accounts payable, accounts receivable, reconciliation, balance sheets, and all the things you can name that have to do with accounting was what my job role involved. I was hired to work for their home health care department. In that department, what you do is send employees to work with the elderly in their homes.

Even though I studied accounting, it was a great thing for me to work in healthcare. After I was part of that organization for less than a year, I was promoted to manage their office. I was like, *'Oh my God!!'* I was so amazed when my boss called me in the office, and she said, *"Jocelyn, you show me so much enthusiasm about yourself. You never say no to anything. You are always hungry to learn. You learned so much here in such a short period that I think you should be the manager. I think your perfect role should be to manage this office. I don't want to see you assisting in accounting anymore. You have proven to me that you can do more than what you are already doing."*

I cannot describe in words how happy I was, but at the same time, I was scared because I was going to play a different role now. I was going to manage my co-workers, so I was nervous. I recall telling my boss at the time, *"The only thing that I ask you is while I am doing the new role, if you think even for once that I am not doing it as nicely as you expected, don't fire me. You can always pull me back to whatever position you want, but I love my job, and I don't want to lose it."* The reason why I said this to her was that even though she offered that position to me and thought I was worthy of that position; I was not confident if I would be able to do it at the time, yet I took it, nonetheless. I knew I was given the opportunity to prove myself and do better. How could I miss it? My boss saw it in me, and I felt like I could do it. When things like this come to you all of a sudden, consider it God's sign. I thought this is my chance to prove myself. Soon my designation was changed, and I became the manager of the department. I loved the new role just as much.

Working in healthcare is something I am so passionate about because this way, I get to help others. Since my family had fallen prey to a fatal disease, and I have seen them in pain, to me, working in health care was all about helping others not to go through the same pain.

My responsibilities also included making sure all our patients had somebody in their homes, who sought someone's help to function and perform routine tasks like doing the laundry, cooking, and accompany the patient to visiting the doctors. This is what the company that I worked with does under Home Health Care. Being in Home Health Care also is part of helping these people and talking to them on the phone. When you are working in this type of field, you become everything.

You become a social worker, your patients' best friends; you become their psychiatrists and companions at the same time. You need to have all these things in place because the people you are assigned to are very sick, and they can be of any age. You become their family; you even talk to insurance companies for them. There are a lot of people involved, and you have to be in touch with all of them, to be able to manage your respective patient.

You are the one talking to nurses, nurse practitioners, and physical therapists, i.e., so many people from different backgrounds. You are even speaking with speech pathologists because some of the patients don't have a voice for themselves. They have somebody who takes care of them in the form of caregivers and proxies. Therefore, you get involved with a whole new circle of people just to assist someone, and that is something I fell in love with.

Back in the 2000s, I don't remember the exact year, Medicaid Medicare did a big turnaround. They required their patients to enroll in healthcare insurance (MLTC) Managed Long Term Care. Once a patient enrolled themselves for the insurances, I said to myself, 'wait a minute!' this is something new, and it's something I did not know of. Anyway, being a manager for that department, I was also very involved in the billing, and I was required to know whatever it was. Since Medicaid wanted to do change its policy, I had to have knowledge about the subject, which propelled me to go back to school.

I went back and became certified and licensed on that particular subject because even though they were going to train me up for the new upcoming changes, I wanted to have the first-hand knowledge of my own. I was always willing to go back to school, get certified, and learn to become better at overseeing the billing. At that time, I was doing the billing for the company as well as myself. The reason why I was involved in managing and billing at the same time was that my boss trusted me. She trusted me so much with the billing and accounting in that part that she did not want to take it away from me with the new role. Though I was honored to be recognized and trusted so much, it was so overwhelming to work two different jobs. I was practically working seven days a week because besides managing the office on weekdays, I was working through on - calls on the weekends as well. You have to coordinate who you are going to send to the patient. This way, I was playing two different roles.

I was a manager as well as a part-time coordinator because when you work in this field, you have to be prepared for the multi-tasking. Working 7 days per week. Like every other hectic job, it was tiring and frustrating. There were days when I wanted to throw myself off a towel and quit, but you know there are days when you don't feel yourself. You feel like quitting, you feel that you want to leave, you don't want to work there anymore, and you just want to walk out.

Nonetheless, I stayed persistent and continued to learn and work in the healthcare field. I learned how to overcome my stress with time. I learned a lot about customer service. I also learned that there are moments when you are so frustrated, and you get patients who make you even more frustrated, but you have to keep your patience.

You have to be able to listen because your patients might be more frustrated than you are because they are the ones who are sick. I used to calm myself, take a deep breath, and listened to what the patients had to say. I let the person on the other side talk and express themselves while I quietly listened to them. Some of the patients only want you to listen. They want someone to listen because they are sick, and some of them live by themselves. They don't have anybody to talk to. That is one thing I learned working in this field; to help patients, to be able to listen, and to encourage others. After dealing with these patients, I learned my lesson, so when some of them called the office while being angry for whatever reason, I learned how to listen, let them speak first, and be calm all the way until I can express myself to them.

You won't believe it, but I have patients that cursed me out. I still have families that curse me out. I have a family that calls me all kinds of names, but I remain calm and strong. I don't lose my coolness because I know it is only going to hurt me later when I think about it. When you have patients, they are your customers, so they are always right, whether they did wrong or not – this is one more thing that I have learned in this field. One thing I have to say is that I mastered to be patient and calm when it came to my patients, family, and the rest of the people involved in this career.

However, working in this field, you deal with a lot of different types of people. I dealt with a lot of directors and people belonging to different professions. One thing that I have to say is a highlight for me besides my customer service. I am very professional in every way. I am very professional with my attire, the way I dress, and about how I speak to others, especially to the employees working under me. I have a lot of respect for my employees because if they leave, who am I going to have? I am going to be the one doing their job. Even though there is always someone looking for a job I try my best to keep my employees happy. This is something which is a part of my personality, or probably I learned over time through all these professional years.

I always involve my employees and let them give their opinion. It's not only about me; it's about the team and how we work. We can only get better when we, as a team work at the same pace and in the same direction. I feel like I owe this company a lot because I learned so much here, which I am so grateful for. I am especially thankful to the boss that I had, who promoted me at that time. After a few years of working with her, she left that company, and I continued working there.

I remember one of their nurses came to me and said, *"Jocelyn, I want you to learn everything about every department as a manager,"* and that's what I did. I took her advice seriously because I knew it is going to be beneficial for me. Regardless of whether it was going to be beneficial or not, I took her advice, and I used it wisely.

I used to sit down with every department and see what they do and learn. Why? Because I needed to know exactly what the employees were doing so that I could address problems well. I needed to be in their shoes to be able to get this knowledge. I need to feel what they are going through to be able to resolve better. As a manager, I needed to have a clear picture of what was going on with the business, and as an accountant, I needed to know where was all the money was going. There are so many responsibilities that you have as a manager, but I always enjoyed my job.

I recall, since I went through all the directors, one person came to work in the office to work as a director. I was called a super-woman in this company because I had the knowledge of every operation within the premises of our company. Of course, the director came, and I had to teach him how the company was performing all the tasks; all the places and procedures of how we do things. Everybody was so excited about getting a new director. The person also seemed nice and lovely, and everything was going well. He seemed the kind of person I could get along with.

After the director had been in the company for a while, one day, this person came to the office and said, "*Jocelyn! Can you come to my office?*" and I said, *"Of course!"* then he continued, *"You need to clean my office."* And I was like, *"Excuse me? Say what?"* That person started laughing and asked, *"Did I say anything wrong?"* I said, *"I think you did."* Then he said, *"I asked you to clean my office because the previous office that I worked in, the office manager used to clean my office."* I said, *"Well, you are saying that the office manager where you came from used to clean your office, but in this office, we work differently because I know we have a cleaning person here, and I have never cleaned any office for anyone."*

One thing that I was confident about was that I was promoted to be a manager because I deserved that promotion because I worked hard to get there. I like to be Jocelyn and be promoted because I deserve that promotion. I did not get this position by giving favors to the directors or the VP or for anybody else. That is something I will never ever do. I have never been a kiss ass, and I will never do things out of my scope of practice for my professional reasons to be promoted to any position. Therefore, I said to this person, "*I am very sorry, I will not clean your office. You can find somebody else to do this. As a manager, I cannot accept that any of the employees do it for you as well because that's incorrect. No one should be cleaning your office when we have a cleaning person here. Moreover, I think your job as a person is to keep the area where you work clean.*"

The person got very upset. The next day, he came back to me and said *that he was not happy with my work and wanted me to stay in the office after working hours.* I said, "*But why should I stay in the office after the actual working hours? It's already my time to leave the office. All my work is done, and I have provided all the reports. If there was anything else that I needed to do, I was not aware of it. I work here, five days of the week. I am working at night back home, too. I am working on the weekends, and I am practically giving my blood out to you guys. Come on! Be more considerate. I have a family, and I need to go home as well. If I need to stay here late necessarily, then I will stay, but I am not going to stay here with you alone. I am sure if there is a priority task, there must be more people involved and not just myself, and if it is just myself, you will always let me know in advance so I could make arrangements. If there's any other last-minute task, I will also be glad to do it, but there is nothing pending."*

I guess the person was not feeling too happy about what I said, and he was not really appreciating the work that I was doing. I have been working in that company for years before that person came in, so I decided that I will ignore this person's comments and continue business as usual. I decided not to take him personally and keep doing my job well. Soon, everybody started noticing that this person was very weird, not only with me but with everybody else as well. That's one thing you know when you are working at a place; you want to keep your job; you keep certain things to yourself.

You do not want to say anything because you feel nobody is going to help you, and nobody is going to believe you. We are always afraid to lose our jobs; hence we always forget about the bad experiences. We know what we are doing, and we know all of us can find jobs somewhere else. However, when you already know the place you are working and the employees that you are working with, you don't want to leave that place because of just one person is inconvenient and wants to ruin your life.

Anyway, I started ignoring the person and continued doing my job. One day, this person had some medical procedures, and while he was in the doctor's clinic, he called my office and asked to speak to me. He told me whatever he had to tell me, and I was listening to him patiently. He said to me, *"Oh, I am about to get ready for my procedure. I am lying without clothes, and I am naked. I just have my gown on, and I am trying to remove my gown as well because I am sweating, and I am hot."* I said, *"Excuse me? Don't say that to me. You are not supposed to say things like that to me. This is very unprofessional."* I also said that I considered his act as sexual harassment. He had been harassing me for a while now, but this time, it was sexual harassment. This was the limit for me. Then he said, "The doctors are coming, I need to hang up."

I remember he called me back right away and said, *"Please don't say anything to anyone."* You know, as a human, if you think you said something right to the person, you do not call someone back. That person knew he said something wrong, so he called back right away and asked me not to tell anyone. I remember going to one of their nurses, and saying, *"This is out of control. He just called me and said all these things to me, and at this point, I don't know what to do."* So, the person said, *"Oh, you know how he is. Let him be, let it go, don't say anything. Just ignore whatever happened and keep your mouth shut."*

I honestly did not know what to do. Therefore, I decided to talk to my husband. I told him what happened, and he got furious. He said, *"Wait a minute!"* and I said, "No, just let it be, I don't want to say anything because I don't see any point." I decided to let it go thinking this person is going to stop, but the harassment continued.

One day, he even humiliated me in front of all the staff, and that's when I decided to go to HR. It was like this person had something against me, which I did not really understand because I had nothing against him, and I was helping this person so much. I believe this person was acting like that because he felt threatened by me. He felt that I was more capable than him of doing his job. I recall this person used to encourage me that *"Why don't you get another job somewhere else. It is going to be brighter and bigger."* When I did not take his advice, he decided to make me reach a point where I quit on my own.

Therefore, I went to the (HR) Human Resources and disclosed everything, thinking they are going to do something or they are going to take action against him, but believe it or not, they did not do anything. They did an investigation, and I believe that they went on his side. Upon confronting, he denied everything. Keep in mind that this person knew how to manipulate. He was the type of person that he will cry, change the story, and turn everything around. All of this was enough for me to convince myself that I needed to get another job. I am not enough appreciated here, so I need to get another job; however, before I left the hospital the person resigned.

After working in that company for twelve years, I did not

want to quit because it was very close to my house, ten blocks away from the house. I could have walked there, but sometimes I used to take the train, especially in the winter. I had stayed there for long, but now things were out of hands. Hence, I decided to look for another job. I believe this person was very insecure and believed that I was a competition. He saw me as a threat to his position. However, when I think about it today, I believe it worked out for the best.

Right now, I am working in such a great company. I have been working in this company for five years. Moreover, I am working in the field of health care for more than seventeen years already, and I love working in this field. Besides that, I have a job. The feeling that I am helping people in different ways is just out of this world. I love helping people. After the pain that my family and I went through, I became compassionate and empathetic towards other people and their feelings.

I created a page on Facebook, where I talk about Gardner's Syndrome and educate everyone about its early symptoms and cures. The disease that my family carries is lethal, but I want people to survive as much as they can. I helped a lot of people to understand how this condition works in your body. I get messages from different people and different parts of the world. I help them understand this condition, and this is something I am pleased about. To me, promoting health is very important. Sometimes you promote things, but you do not practice it on your own. I love promoting health because I want people to be healthy, which is regardless of the fact that I do not take care of myself as much. I am not a healthy eater; I eat everything without a thought. I am not good at eating vegetables, but I like to encourage others to do so. I have learned over time that without health, there is no life.

If your family is not healthy, you are not healthy, but sometimes there is nothing you can do about it. To me, working in this field is very special, it doesn't matter in which department I work in the future. I would like to continue working in the field of healthcare. I would love to open a foundation of my own, where I can help others and encourage them to take care of themselves.

I want to encourage people always to prevent themselves from diseases. Keep yourself healthy. I have a lot of things to accomplish in my life, and there are a lot of people out there who need my help and assistance. I want to help others as much as I can. If I have resources to do it, I will, especially in health care. Looking forward, if I have the opportunity to open that foundation through which I can help people with supplies like wheelchairs, diapers, etc. I will launch it without a thought. There are a lot of families who cannot afford it, not only in this country but in so many other countries as well. One thing I have to say is that even though I don't have the foundation, I try as much as I can to help the people in need. I don't want to limit myself to the boundaries. I want to serve humanity as much as I can.

Sometimes it's not only medication. There are a lot of things that people need, and they are not able to afford it. Sometimes people don't have a wheelchair or even crutches to walk. It will be like a dream come true for me to help people as such and make their lives easier, which I do as well without the foundation. That's what I chose for my career. I could be anything from a simple accountant to a great writer, but I chose this because this is something, I love the most. When I see people doing better because of me, it fills me with life and energy, and all my tiredness fades away.

I have been working in the health care field for more than two decades, and I will continue to do that whenever I have the opportunity.

Chapter 13
Nothing Lasts Forever:
Live in the Present

Who is a hero to you? They are probably someone who is brave, has outstanding achievements and noble qualities, and whose courage we admire. A hero is someone who comes back at adversity through pillars of strength, and loves unconditionally, without asking anything in return. I have known a hero who loved to give, whose demonstrations, decisions, and behaviors were all ethical and unquestionable.

He was a legendary figure with rare abilities. He worked his life in many ways for the greatest of others and to be able to serve others. That is the man that I call my father, my hero, my Papi. We often assume that heroes live forever, and nothing can happen to them because they are so kind, generous, and always giving. But guess what? I was completely wrong. Nothing in this world lasts forever, not even the heroes who are the saviors of the world. In my eyes and those of my siblings, grandchildren, aunts, uncles, nephews and nieces', my father is the greatest man the world has ever seen. We all believed that he was the bravest man and that he could survive through just anything. We all thought that he was the rock, the person who will never break and will always stay strong, being there for all of us. Regardless of anything, he never said no, sacrificed his life to give it to others, and us especially. He indeed was brave; he never showed how weak he got when we lost our mother, his wife. He never let anyone know how sad he was when my oldest sister departed from this world. However, we are humans, and from the moment that we are born, we are exposed to getting sick, break, and go through things in this journey of life. Amid all of this, we sometimes forget that heroes who go through all this have feelings too, they are also humans, and they can break just like humans usually do.

I want to dedicate this chapter to my hero, my beloved father. I got very attached to my father, who I call "Papi," after my mother died. I would spend time with him as much as I could, and we loved each other's company. My father was a great dancer, which I mentioned in the early chapters as well. I was one of his dancing partner's. From the youngest kid to the oldest person, everyone in my family knew and still knows how to dance on all types of music.

However, there is one particular dance form that my father loved, which is called "salsa." He taught all of us how to dance "salsa." A person who dances "salsa" is called "Rumbero" in Spanish, depending on the skills that this person possesses. My father was not a Rumbero-type who went to a dancing school and learned how to dance. He learned salsa from the street, on his own, and by going to parties. I must say he was a great self-learner because he still was very good at it. Papi taught me the same way – to dance just like one "Rumbera" as well. I dance salsa like crazy; my father believed I am a great dancer, which I love and appreciated.

My father and I had one day in specific when we used to dance salsa; it was Friday. Every Friday, my father and I used to meet, and it was always fun. We used to dance, have some beers, and laugh a lot. Besides Fridays, we often also used to meet on Saturdays either at my brother's house or my father's house. Every time my father and I were together, we would play music and dance to it. This way, every time my father was around, an ordinary day would turn into a happy day. He loved to play music, so whenever the house was quiet, he would say, *"Where is the radio? Let's play some music.*" We danced like there was no tomorrow, not caring about anything, no matter where we were. Even if we were out at a restaurant and they played music, we used to get up and start dancing. My father used to drink lots of beer on the weekends on his days off from work and he smoked every day. One day, he started acting very strangely, and we thought it was just him acting that way, maybe because he was drunk. We kind of ignored, but sometimes he used to start acting too weirdly for us to ignore. Then I used to ask him, *"Are you drunk?"* And he would say, *"No, I did not drink anything today."* Of course, his behavior spoke the opposite.

My siblings and I started to notice his strange behavior, and we would ask each other about what went on with him. It got to the point that we started telling him to go to the doctor and get himself checked. One day, we all sat and decided that we were going to make an appointment for my father to see the doctor. The problem was, he remembered nothing about his strange behavior since he used to be too drunk. We were very much concerned about it. My father was the kind of person who never went to the hospital. Like the majority of the men, he did not like going to the doctors.

He thought he was tough and did not need any medications. As a result, every time we used to mention it to him that he needed to go and get himself checked because he was not a young person anymore. He was in his sixties; he would not pay attention to any of the things that we said.

Besides dancing, my father was athletic. He was able to play every sport, but his favorite sport was scuba diving at a young age. He exercises every single day, and that was a part of his routine. He had a fabulous physique; he was very muscular, tough, and physically solid. Therefore, he relied on that. He would say, *"I am doing exercise all the time. I am taking care of myself. I drink a lot of natural drinks, so don't worry about me."* He used to make a lot of natural drinks on his own. Moreover, he did not eat so much meat; he only ate fish and seafood, so his diet was quite healthy. All of this is the reason he thought nothing was going to happen to him.

One day in February 2016, I came home from work in the afternoon, and my father was waiting for me. He looked strange, very unusual. I said to him, *"Bendicion Papi!"* That's a phrase that we use to greet our parents or older person. No matter if it's your aunt or your grandparents, you can say it because it means 'bless you!' and they would reply to you, 'God bless you, too!' So, I said that to my father, and when he looked at me, I noticed that he looked very confused. Right away, I went to the computer, opened Google to look for symptoms, and started asking him questions. I was looking for the reason behind his strange behavior. He was mumbling. I could not understand what he was saying. I asked him, *"Did you drink today?"* and he said, *"No!"* I asked if he had gone to work, and he said yes. I replied, *"Then what's wrong with you?"* He said, *"Nothing."* I could not understand what he was saying, so I had to get very close to him to be able to understand what he was trying to say.

At that time, "Papi" was sixty-four years old, so I said to him, *"Something must be wrong with you."* All he said to me was, *"I am going home." "You cannot go home like this. You don't look fine.* I know there is something wrong with you." I replied. He said, *"I want to go home." "Can I take you home?"* I asked, he said, *"No! I want to walk."* He was still mumbling.

As soon as he left, I called my sister and told her, *"Papi does not look too good. I think we need to call 911,"* because when I did my research, all the symptoms that I found pointed towards he was going to get a stroke. My sister got so scared because my father was a strong man and he did not want us to tell him what to do. He was that type of macho man. He would say, 'I am the one who says whatever I have to say. You guys don't tell me what to do.' So, we used to joke around with him. Despite all of this, my father and I were like best friends. I used to tell my father a lot of things about myself. Of course, there were certain things I could not speak to him about, but we were very close. He was very close to my brother and sisters as well.

I told my sister, *"Listen! If you are scared to call the ambulance because of his reaction, I will call, and I am also going over there."* I get very nervous in such situations, so I said to her, *"If you do not call 911, then I am going to call my husband to go over there and call the ambulance and the police if it is necessary because he does not look too good."* My sister was okay. I decided to go after our father, but then I was afraid he is going to refuse and create problems, so I decided to stay back. I did not know what to do. When my husband came home, he found me shaking nervously and got worried, he asked, *"What's going on?"* and I said, *"I don't know, but my father does not look too good. We need to call 911. My sister is afraid to call, so, please. I want to go there, and I will go with you."* My husband said, *"No, you stay back. You are already too nervous. He is probably going to start acting tough. You know how your father is, so I am going to go over there by myself."*

My husband headed over there, and while he was on his way, I called my sister and said, *"Listen! Ask Papi what his name is? What is his date of birth?"* When she asked him what his name and DOB is, he remembered neither of them. I was worried that he is going to collapse right there in the house, and it is going to be worse. My husband arrived at the house right away and called 911. My father was refusing to go to the hospital as expected, so we had to call the cops. He was confused and did not know where he was. Therefore, we needed to take him to the hospital forcefully.

When the cops came in, it was a female and a male. The female cops talked to my father. She persuaded him to go to the hospital, and he walked out of the house on his own. He did not have to be forced. By the time my father got to the hospital, he did not know where he was. He had lost his mind and was utterly perplexed. I remember that day I was cooking, and I could not leave the food halfway, plus I was so nervous about seeing my father going into an ambulance. Whereas, my nephew went to the hospital with my father and my husband. Two hours later, after running certain tests, the doctors came back and said to my nephew, *"We have a piece of bad news for you guys. We think that there is a tumor in his brain."*

When my nephew called and told me the bad news, my whole world collapsed. I said to myself, 'Oh my God! What am I going to do now? I cannot believe that my hero is sick. How can this happen to him?' I could not believe my hero was sick. Right away, I finished cooking, got dressed, and almost ran to the hospital. The hospital was not so far from where I lived, but I could not drive because I was too nervous. My husband came back from the hospital and took me there.

My father looked so weak. My heart shattered, watching the same man who would dance like there was no tomorrow, lying helpless on that hospital bed. I could not leave my father's side, so I stayed in the hospital that night. The same night, the doctors came back and thought my father had meningitis, which is a disease that swells the protective membranes covering the brain and spinal cord. This was the reason why his brain was not working properly. Meningitis is very contagious. Therefore, he was isolated in a room where we had to wear gowns and masks to visit him.

The doctors told us that we have to be very precautious when going inside that room. My father opened his eyes. He was looking at us and still did not know where he was. He did not recognize any of us present in the room. After staying in the hospital for one night, I came home in the morning, took a shower, and went to work. When my boss saw me, she said, *"Jocelyn you don't look too great, what's wrong?"* I had just started a job at that time, so I was very responsible.

Even though I was there for about six months, I did not want to call out. I was one of the operation managers, and I did not want to put my responsibilities on anyone else. Even though I was going through such a hard time, I showed up at work. My boss was such a nice person; she right away said, *"No, Jocelyn! You need to go home. You look very tired. I came to know about your father. You can go back home and rest."*

I did not go back home, but back to the hospital where my father was. They took him out of that room because they re-ran a few tests and said, *"He does not have meningitis, it looks like there is a tumor in his brain that is affecting his memory. We cannot say exactly if that is the case, we are going to run more tests and then make a decision the doctors said."* My father was admitted into the hospital on Monday, and on the evening of Tuesday, the doctor called my sister and said, *"We had run some more tests on your father, and we have to speak to the family. We have made a decision, but I want everyone to be present here."* The whole family was there the next morning, including my siblings, nephews, cousins, and aunts, we were all there.

My father was awake at that time. Four doctors came in and asked if everybody was there and we said yes. At this point, my father could not make a decision for himself. He just knew we were related to him, but he did not know what kind of relationship we shared. He just had that feeling that we are a part of his family, but he could not recognize that we were his children.

The doctors then said something that I never wanted to hear. I never wanted to hear that my father was sick. In my mind, I believed he would never be sick or so sick. In my mind, he was going to get discharged soon to be there to protect us as he did. I always had that in my mind that my hero is strong and always here for us, and he is not going to break. The doctors said, *"Unfortunately, we have gathered you all here to ask for your permission. We are going to run an emergency surgery on your father because the tumor that he has in his head is cancerous."*

When I heard that it was cancer, I passed out. I could not handle it; I could not believe my hero, my father, my "Papi," had cancer in the brain. I almost hit my head on one of the tables in the room, thank God my nephew was there, and he caught me on time. My whole body broke down onto the floor. I remember when the doctor was talking to us, I felt like the entire ceiling was coming down on top of me. When I woke up, I was lying down on a hospital bed, surrounded by doctors, where they were checking me and found my heartbeat and blood pressure was extremely high.

I was pale, and they were asking me if I was okay. They needed to admit me, but I said, *"No! Please, I want to be there with my father. I don't want to be admitted. I am just in shock to know that my father has cancer. This is something I cannot believe. Heroes don't get sick, so how can my father be sick? How did this happen?"* I was asking all these questions while the doctors were checking me. My father always used to call me dramatic. If he was able to express himself at the moment, he would go like, 'What happened to her? She is probably doing her drama.' I am very expressive. I don't hide anything, and I am not afraid to show my feelings. If I am sad, happy, or even upset, you would know just by looking at my face. I smile through pain and sadness, but you can look at my face and tell that it's not the true smile, and I am not happy. Anyway, they checked me, and I told them I was fine. They gave me medications to calm me down. When I got better, the doctor said that my father needs to get surgery as soon as possible.

My brother, sister, nephew, and I signed all the documentation and gave our permission for the surgery to begin, and so it did. The tumor that my father had in his brain is called Glioblastoma. These types of tumors affect more men than women. It's usually between the age of 50 and 60. It also affects children, but hardly affects people belonging to the middle-aged group and under.

The next day after my father had the surgery, the doctor came to speak to us. He said everything was fine, and they had removed the tumor. He said there was a tiny part that they did not remove because it would have taken his memory away almost 100%. Thankfully, everything went smoothly. He also added that they had removed as much as they could. The first question I asked was, "What is the stage of cancer?" They said that the stage of the cancer was stage four. I immediately asked, *"What are the chances of survival for my father?"* They said, *"A year or two."*

Oh my Gosh! I cannot describe in words how painful it was to hear that from the doctors. It was as if someone had crushed glass and put it in my ears. I start running like crazy. I thought I was going to throw myself down the window. I did not know what to do. I wished for someone to appear and tell me my hero was not going to die. The doctor said, *"Don't worry, because we are going to treat him. We are going to give him medications, and we are going to do everything we can to help your father to live. However, the tumor is very aggressive. I don't want to scare you guys, but it is the truth."*

I said to him, *"I just want you to speak the truth. If I know the truth, I can be able to help my father better. If you hide it from me, it will be of no use.* It's *better that you tell me the truth even if it hurts us. Just speak to us what exactly is going on."* The doctor said, *"Usually, the people who have this type of tumor in their brain that we treat, they don't survive because these tumors are very aggressive."*

Anyhow, despite all the risks, the surgery went well. My father could not walk in the beginning, so they started giving him physical therapies. He came back to himself. Despite all the horrible news, it was my 40th birthday coming up at that time. I remember we celebrated my birthday the best possible way. It was so beautiful. We went to a restaurant. Of course, I danced with my father that night.

We did not want to give him any liquor because he recently had surgery just a couple of weeks before. However, at one point, I said to everyone, *"You know what? Let's get drunk, let's dance, and let's do everything that is going to make us happy."* We ended up doing all of it. It was a beautiful day. The following week, my sister's birthday came, but that day my father was not feeling well, so he could not go with us to celebrate.

A whole year passed, and again, 'papi" started to look like he was not in a conscious state of mind. He did not know where he was, so again we took him to the hospital, only to find out that the tumor had come back. He had to go through surgery again, but this time along, he did not come back to being the same man he was. He started to deteriorate rapidly. The doctors said, *"Unfortunately, there is nothing else we can do. We have to put him under the Hospice Care."* I said, *"No, you are not putting my father into Hospice. If you guys are not going to do anything, we will take him to another hospital. I am not going to let anything happen to my father. I am going to do my research, and I am going to try to save my father because my hero cannot die."*

Therefore, they gave me all the papers, and when my father got discharged, I took him to another hospital in Manhattan. They were able to help him a little bit. My father was resistant to get chemotherapies and any type of treatment. When we used to put pressure on him to go to the hospital, *he would say, "Whenever I fall, I am not going to get back up."* He was so strong, so we were not habitual of listening to this from him. We always used to get mad at him for saying such things. We used to say, *"No. You are going to get back up. You are very strong. Nothing is going to happen to you."*

It was March 2017 when I took my father to the hospital in Manhattan to get a second opinion. After he was treated, they decided to give him chemotherapy. He had only one chemotherapy treatment. He said he is not going back again. We respected his wishes, so we said, "Okay, don't do it, but we want you to help yourself." That was the time when my father decided to become homebound. He did not want to come out at all, not even to my house like he used to. He wanted to sleep all the time. I believe he was very depressed. He forgot my name and even my sister's. Gradually, he forgot a lot of things.

The symptoms did not stay limited to "papi's memory loss" only. He was getting weaker day by day. He was able to walk, but then one day, he woke up and started limping. He started losing his vision. He used to call me by his sister's name. So many more things like these started to happen, which indicated his worsening condition. Every Friday, I used to go see him, but sometimes I used to get late coming back home from work.

On days like those, he used to ask my sister, *"What happened to the lady? She always comes here late on Fridays. Doesn't she know I am tired? When she comes, she is so loud. She comes with a beer, plays music, and she always parties. I don't understand what's wrong with that lady."* He thoroughly forgot that we used to party on Fridays, but I continued our tradition. I wanted my father to return to how he used to be, which is why I used to do everything he used to do; everything that could bring back his old self, but unfortunately, his health was only declining. Despite everything, I used to play music, especially the ones he loved the most. Sometimes, he remembered. He used to get up and ask, *"What? Do you want to dance?"* and I would say yes. I used to hug my father, dancing and crying. He used to say to me, *"What happened to you? You don't look okay?"* but I *always denied. "I just got something inside my eyes; that is why they are teary," I said.* He used to laugh, and I said, *"Are you tired?"* Because he tried to dance like he used to, but he couldn't because of his hip. His body was not the same. Cancer in his brain was affecting his mobility, and he could not move his left side properly.

My father got so weak in no time that he was not able to pick up the spoon to eat anymore. He forgot everybody's name. From the moment he got sick in 2016, we thought he should stay home and not work, and we'd take care of everything. My father was the breadwinner, of course. He was so independent that he never wanted anyone to do anything for him. He was always giving to us and barely taking anything. He was always bringing me things, from Christmas and birthday gifts to medications when I was sick. He was selfless. Unfortunately, my father became weak. The reason why his condition worsened much quicker was that he refused to go to the hospital, I believe. He needed to get the medication because he was in pain. He would never express his pain, but we knew because his face used to get red. He looked different when he was in pain. We enrolled my father under the Hospice program so he could be comfortable on his last days, we arranged all the medication that was needed. We knew he was in pain just by looking at him.

My father was very reserved. He never used to show us any weakness. He always used to say that he was one hundred percent fine. Probably he was breaking inside because all his children were sick. When "papi" got sick, I became hopeless. I used to say he was my only supporter when my brother and sisters were all sick. I always thought that I am probably going to be left alone with my father in this world, but life can turn around. You never can expect anything because you never know what is going to happen next in our life. I always thought I would be left alone with him, but who knew he was going to be the one to leave us first? The man that was always there for me and all of us had to bid his final goodbye. Then came a week when my father fell very sick. It was Saturday night when he went to the bathroom, but he could not walk properly. He was reluctant to take help and still wanted to be independent. Therefore, he went to the bathroom on his own; he fell and could not get back up. My youngest sister found him alone with my nephews' wife.

They got him out of the bathroom. He looked more confused. My sister called the nurse, and she told my sister to call 911. My sister called my nephew right away, who was not home at the time, and right away, he came home and took my father to the hospital. Then my sister called me as well to let me know what had happened. I got so anxious; my nephew told me to reach him at the hospital, so I did.

My father remembered nothing about his fall. My sister and I took turns to stay in the hospital. We could not leave him alone in the hospital. I remember calling my boss and telling her that I was not coming to work because I had to stay with my father. I told her my father was in a critical stage of life, and all of us siblings stayed together with my father. Unfortunately, my youngest brother was waiting to get an intestine transplant. And he was called right at that moment to rush to the hospital. Can you imagine that? What worse could we go through? Meanwhile, my father got discharged, and we took him to his home on Tuesday. From there, my father started to decay. Fridays now reminded me of my best and my worst days because Friday was the last day I saw my father alive. The hospital wanted to keep him there.

They asked me if I want to keep him in the hospital because he was living in the last stage. Before they sent him home, the doctors came to speak to us. They said, *"Unfortunately, your father is very sick. Cancer has spread to his lungs, so there is no way he can survive."* I was unable to understand what was going on because they had first said that he had a blockage in his heart, and he could get a heart attack. Then they came back and said that cancer had spread through his lungs, too.

I didn't leave my father from the moment he went to the hospital. I was always by his side at all times. I only came home to sleep by one or two hours in the morning because I needed to get my child ready to go to school the next day.

After that, I would go back to the hospital where my father was; however, I took my father to his home. We were all there in his room when the nurse came in. It was Friday, again, and I said to the nurse, *"I want you to tell me the truth. How much time does my father have? Because he is breathing weird, he is breathing very heavily, and he has a lot of fever…and the fever does not go down. Even though it's difficult, I want you to tell me what exactly is going on. I want to be by his side every moment."* She said, *"Okay, since you guys are so honest with me, so open with me, I am going to tell you the truth. Your father has no more than twenty-four hours to live."*

I felt like the sky was falling on me. It was as if someone had taken away the roof from my head and the ground beneath my feet. I felt the warmth of a father's love going away while I stood barefooted in the cold. What was I going to do with my life now? There was no point in life without him. These nurses, since they deal with such patients daily, they most likely know the time a person has to live.

They are not God, but because they have the experience, they can tell. She then gave me a few tips on when somebody is dying, how their body looks. Things that happen in a person's body when they are departing. She told me all these things, and obviously, we all started crying badly.

She stayed with us for a little bit, gave us a lot of courage. She asked us if we wanted to pray, and we said, "Yes." So, we prayed together, and from that moment, I just did not want to leave my father's side. I stayed with my father. All his grandchildren also came in, and so did the rest of the family. Meanwhile, my brother was in the hospital, getting his surgery. We gathered around my father, watching him helplessly leave this world. That is the hardest part for a person to witness – your loved one, your hero, the one you thought was never going to leave your side, the one you believed was so strong that nothing could happen to him was leaving you slowly, wow! That's life, and it is very painful for me.

Friday night! I told everyone who was present in the room that I want to drink beer. I asked my husband to buy me a beer, so he did. I even gave beer to my father, and he drank it. Everyone thought I was crazy and questioned why I was doing all of that. I told them just to let me be who I was with him and requested them not to take that away from me already. I asked them to understand my wishes, as my father was going to depart soon. I drank a couple of beers, and gave some to "papi," too.

He was not speaking to us nor even looking at us. I played music that he liked. I was by his side. I did not want to leave him; I wanted to sleep right next to him that night, but they did not let me. They said it's not good to sleep next to someone who is dying. I was persistent to sleep next to him because I wanted to hug him for one last time, but they did not allow me.

The next morning was hard. We were all there. I remember telling my father, *"Don't leave us!"* When I understood that nothing could change the reality, I said, *"You know if you are bound to leave, there is one thing I want to say, we are going to be okay. Don't you worry about us. Just always know how much we love you. We have always told you that you are the best father anyone can have, you are our hero. No man in my eyes will ever be better than you. You are the best man that I ever met in my life. I love you!"*

We all said our little things to him. At one point, I was so tired I fell asleep. My younger sister spent the rest of the night with my father. However, she couldn't handle it anymore. I saw her falling asleep, as well. I told her I would stay with him. This happened around 6:30 a.m. on a Saturday morning. Then came the time for him to depart. It was November 18, 2017, at 9:18 in the morning. I was holding my father's forehead because he was having so much fever. I was putting cold towels to help the fever go down. The fever started going down. I had said to my sister, *"When the fever goes down, he is going to die,"* and it was happening right in front of my eyes. He started breathing heavily, and then it slowed down. When he took his second-deep breath, I got up and ran out of the room. I said, *"I cannot see my father leaving."* I ran away and called his cousin, who was there in the house and said, *"I think that is it! He is going to die."* Right after that, he took his last breaths and then went numb.

His cousin then went to his room and announced my father's death, alone with my husband. That was one of the worst parts of my life. It was as if I was living a dark nightmare. When one of your parents leave, you feel the whole world collapsing. You lose the ability to see reality. My heart was just not accepting what had happened. I felt like I was sinking in the ground, and my life was over losing my hero, the person that I thought will never die. He taught me so many things, but most importantly, the value of helping and checking up on others. I could have saved him, I thought, but because he never went to the hospital to get himself checked, we lost him. We often don't want to go to the hospital because we are afraid of the bad news.

Sometimes, yet, if you go on time and get yourself checked regularly, you can prevent so many things from happening. Maybe if my father had gone to the hospital on time, they would have cut the tumor on time. It was tiny, but it was already stage-four. They probably could have taken it out at stage one. They would have been able to help him, and maybe he could have lived longer.

I was being selfish when I wished for him to live longer. Besides, we all have to leave this world one day. I had lost my mother, my oldest sister, my baby, my father now, as well as my grandparents, cousins, and uncle I was so attached to. What I learned from losing "papi" is that we must enjoy ourselves with our loved ones as much as we can. I have to say I myself have gotten along well with others, and I always try to keep a great relationship. I have had enough losses to come to realize that we are here just for a moment; we all have a time frame. Sometimes we don't pay close attention to that. We have a day destined for us to die. Within that timeframe, we have to do great things, so the world remembers us in their good books. We are not perfect; we make mistakes, and sometimes we hurt people. However, we need to be able to say to the person 'I am sorry' and ensure we do not repeat the same mistake again. In my life, I always hoped that nothing ever ends, but I realized that things do end; everything does eventually.

I myself am trying to understand that sometimes we get mad at our loved ones, and we have a hard time to say sorry. Often, we have a hard time appreciating what people around us do for us because most of the time, we focus more on the bad side than the good side of theirs. When someone you dislike or don't get along well with is dying, you realize their goods surpass their beds, but it's too late to appreciate then. I am learning to appreciate people and their presence while they are breathing and are part of my life. I don't have any issues telling somebody that I made a mistake, or I love them and appreciate what they do.

I am very polite and full of imperfections as well, but I will tell you things as they are. We need to learn how to say those small things to others. I appreciate life because I do not know when it is going to end, and we never know when it is our last conversation with someone. Appreciate what you have and your life while you are living it. It is not going to stay this way forever.

Everything has an expiration date. If you love food, you must appreciate it before it goes bad. If you like a product that you use for your hair, makeup, or anything, you will make use of it and value it while it's in good shape because you know it has an expiration day. However, everything that expires is replaced with new things, but not humans. I learned this lesson the hard way that nothing lasts forever. But one thing I must say is that I am very proud of the family God has given me; my mother, my father, my brother and sisters, my nephews, and the family I created with my husband (i.e., our children and us). If I were be to reincarnated, I would like the same family again.

We have to enjoy every moment of our life as much as we can. I have learned now to live day by day while valuing people who are there for me. I know tomorrow is not a promise. I can be here today, and anything can happen to me tomorrow.

There are moments when we want to curse the life out of the other person, but we have to learn how to control ourselves, knowing that nothing lasts forever. Live trying to be the best of ourselves. It's hard to grow up with all these ups and downs in life, but still, I walk with my head up. I get up in the morning, dress nicely, do my makeup, and act like nothing is happening to me. I act strong even though I feel empty on the inside. My heart does not beat the same way, and I can never be the happiest I used to be.

This is my story; it began with me losing my mother and ends with me losing my very last hope, my savior, my hero, "papi." So, appreciate your parents while you can. Tell them that you love them every single day. Thank them for their sacrifices and love, for you never know what they go through just to see you smile. Live every moment with them to the fullest because you never know what the next day brings. Believe me, when I say, there is no life without them, and nothing is ever going to be the same when they leave. The regret that comes with it is worst, so never take them for granted. Whoever I am today, the lessons I have learned is because of my parents, and the life God has chosen for me to live. I am strong because being strong was not a choice but the only option that I had, and that's how I know how to value life. I love to inspire others. I don't talk about certain things of my life with others very much because I don't want them to feel pitiful about it. I just want others to learn from my story. I want them to learn that when someone leaves, you can still live, smile, and be happy, but at the same time, you need to cry. You need to let it out and free yourself from the pain. Don't hold your emotions inside. Remember your body will react and will give you signs. Listen to your body and what your body needs to tell you. That is how I survive. I have to give credit for this to my father because he taught me how to be strong at a very early age and how to be able to walk with my head up and smile, regardless of what is going on in my life. To learn how to clean my tears and walk like nothing is happening.

Not everyone is supposed to know what we are going through. I want to thank him for making me the woman that I am today. Life is like a book, and sometimes I don't know how to read it. We are born asking, and we die without an answer. Sometimes I ask myself, *where I'm going to be, what is my destiny in this life, and what is going to happen next?* But I don't know what I'm going to find at the end. At the end of this book, I want you to remember that sometimes you may think that you have got it worst, but there are people out there who are going through more painful things and situations than you are. When you compare, you say, 'Well, my life is not as bad as I thought it is.'

Trust me when I say each one of us is born with a set of sufferings and problems to bear, but yes, we must learn to fight each of them. And yes, we are all special in our own ways, and if you look around, you will know that the problems that others are going through are much bigger than yours. Therefore, you must always be grateful despite the ups and downs because that is life. As the name implies, goals in life are those goals we set to achieve a dream. Remember to be happy within you, no one else will make you happy as you will and no one else will love you as you love yourself. That's one thing I have to learn the hard way. Once you love yourself and have that courage and confidence, nothing can stop you to conquer the world and all your dreams. Remember to follow your brain and then listen to your heart.

Those goals can be short-or-long-term, depending on their magnitude and the situations that affect our existence. Basically, its purpose is to give meaning or purpose to our existence. I will continue on the journey that God has prepared for me, and live every moment like it is the last, because every moment is just one moment, and even if you repeat it one thousand times, that moment will never be the same. There are moments when I question myself and ask why I have to live this life. I answer myself, "Life is beautiful." It is indeed, and I will enjoy every aspect of it.

Just remember that some of us are born strong and others have to become strong. I was not born to be strong, but I learn to fight every battle that came my way despite all the facts that life can bring. I am a true fighter and I am strong; I was made strong with each challenge that came my way to help me grow mentally and emotionally. I will move forward with my head high and walk with lots of confidence. I will show everyone that my strength cannot be denied. I am a woman who has been through many storms and I have survived!

"For nothing is impossible with God."

(Luke 1:37)

BLESSED TO BE SKIPPED

Lightning Source UK Ltd.
Milton Keynes UK
UKHW012152190821
389154UK00001B/41